Career Guidance

A HANDBOOK FOR POLICY MAKERS

ORGANISATION FOR ECONOMIC CO-OPERATION AND DEVELOPMENT

EUROPEAN COMMISSION

ORGANISATION FOR ECONOMIC CO-OPERATION AND DEVELOPMENT

Pursuant to Article 1 of the Convention signed in Paris on 14th December 1960, and which came into force on 30th September 1961, the Organisation for Economic Co-operation and Development (OECD) shall promote policies designed:

- to achieve the highest sustainable economic growth and employment and a rising standard of living in member countries, while maintaining financial stability, and thus to contribute to the development of the world economy;
- to contribute to sound economic expansion in member as well as non-member countries in the process of economic development; and
- to contribute to the expansion of world trade on a multilateral, non-discriminatory basis in accordance with international obligations.

The original member countries of the OECD are Austria, Belgium, Canada, Denmark, France, Germany, Greece, Iceland, Ireland, Italy, Luxembourg, the Netherlands, Norway, Portugal, Spain, Sweden, Switzerland, Turkey, the United Kingdom and the United States. The following countries became members subsequently through accession at the dates indicated hereafter: Japan (28th April 1964), Finland (28th January 1969), Australia (7th June 1971), New Zealand (29th May 1973), Mexico (18th May 1994), the Czech Republic (21st December 1995), Hungary (7th May 1996), Poland (22nd November 1996), Korea (2th December 1996) and the Slovak Republic (14th December 2000). The Commission of the European Communities takes part in the work of the OECD (Article 13 of the OECD Convention).

EUROPEAN COMMISSION

The European Commission is the executive body of the European Union responsible for implementing and managing EU policy. Working in close partnership with the other European institutions and with the governments of the 25 Member States, its roles include making proposals for new legislation and acting as the guardian of the EU treaties to ensure that European legislation is applied correctly. The administrative structure of the Commission reflects the scope of its responsibilities within the European Union. The Directorate General for Education and Culture is one of 36 directorates-general and specialised services.

Publié en français sous le titre :

L'orientation professionnelle
GUIDE PRATIQUE POUR LES DÉCIDEURS

The views expressed are purely those of the authors and may not, and in any circumstances, be regarded as stating an official position of the European Commission, the OECD or of the governments of their member countries

Foreword

This publication arises from major reviews of national career guidance policies conducted by the OECD and the European Commission during 2001-2003. Australia, Austria, Canada, the Czech Republic, Denmark, Finland, Germany, Ireland, Korea, Luxembourg, the Netherlands, Norway, Spain and the United Kingdom took part in the OECD review. The European Centre for the Development of Vocational Training (CEDEFOP) gathered data from Belgium, France, Greece, Iceland, Italy, Portugal and Sweden for the European Commission, and the European Training Foundation (ETF) gathered data from Bulgaria, Cyprus, Estonia, Hungary, Latvia, Lithuania, Malta, Poland, Romania, Slovakia and Slovenia. A parallel review by the World Bank was conducted in 2003 in Chile, the Philippines, Poland, Romania, Russia, South Africa and Turkey. In each country the reviews assessed how the organisation, management and delivery of career guidance services contribute to the implementation of lifelong learning and active labour market policies.

The OECD and the European Commission co-operated in planning the reviews, used a common survey instrument (initially designed for use by the 14 countries taking part in the OECD review, and also used as the basis for the World Bank reviews), shared experts and members of review teams, and jointly commissioned expert papers to inform their assessment of key issues. This co-operation has resulted in a unique set of data on national approaches to career guidance services. A number of common messages emerged from the reviews about deficiencies in national career guidance services. Many examples of good practice exist in the countries that were reviewed. Nevertheless there are major gaps between how services are organised and delivered on the one hand and some key public policy goals on the other. Access to services is limited, particularly for adults. Too often services fail to develop people's career management skills, but focus upon immediate decisions. Training and qualification systems for those who provide services are often inadequate or inappropriate. Co-ordination between key ministries and stakeholders is poor. The evidence base is insufficient to allow proper steering of services by policy makers, with inadequate data being available on costs, benefits, client characteristics or outcomes. And in delivering services insufficient use is made of ICT and other cost-effective ways to meet client needs more flexibly.

This publication gives policy makers clear, practical tools that can be used to address these problems. It encompasses the major policy domains involved in developing a comprehensive framework for lifelong guidance systems: meeting the career guidance needs of young people and of adults; widening access to career guidance; improving career information; staffing and funding career guidance services; and improving strategic leadership. Within each of these areas the publication:

✓   Sets out the key challenges that policy makers face in trying to improve career guidance services;

✓   Provides examples of good practice and of effective responses to these challenges, drawing upon research conducted in 36 OECD and European countries;

✓   Lists the questions that policy makers need to ask themselves in responding to these challenges; and

✓   Provides practical options that they can use in order to improve policy.

Material for the publication was prepared by Professor Ronald Sultana of the University of Malta and Professor Tony Watts of the United Kingdom's National Institute for Careers Education and Counselling, both of whom had extensive involvement in the OECD and European Commission reviews. Within the OECD preparation of the publication was supervised by Richard Sweet, and within the European Commission by staff of the Directorate General, Education and Culture. It is published under the responsibility of the Secretary-General of the OECD and the Director General for Education and Culture, European Commission.

Table of Contents

EXECUTIVE SUMMARY

Well planned and well organised career guidance services are increasingly important. Countries in the OECD and the European Union are implementing lifelong learning strategies, as well as policies to encourage the development of their citizens' employability. To be successfully implemented, such strategies and policies require citizens to have the skills to manage their own education and employment. They require all citizens to have access to high quality information and advice about education, training and work. Yet often the gap between how career guidance services are delivered and the goals of public policy is wide. The aim of this handbook is to help policy makers within OECD countries and the European Union to develop effective policies for career guidance: in education, training and employment. It has been developed by the European Commission and the OECD in response to on-going changes in education, training and employment policies. In Europe these changes are expressed in the Lisbon (2000) goals of making Europe the most competitive knowledge-based economy and society in the world by 2010, marked by social cohesion. The handbook is based on international reviews of policies for career guidance undertaken by the OECD, by the European Centre for the Development of Vocational Training, by the European Training Foundation, and by the World Bank. In clear and simple language it sets out for policy makers in education, training and employment settings:

➢ Challenges that they face in making sure that career guidance services can meet public policy goals;

➢ Questions that they need to ask themselves in responding to these challenges;

➢ Some of the options that are open to them for the delivery of career guidance within a lifelong learning and active employability framework; and

➢ Some examples of effective responses, drawn from OECD and European Union countries.

The handbook covers four broad policy themes: Improving career guidance for young people; Improving career guidance for adults; Improving access to career guidance; and Improving the systems that support career guidance.

Improving Career Guidance for Young People

To improve career guidance for young people, policy makers must address challenges in compulsory schooling, in upper secondary schooling, in tertiary education, and for young people at risk. There are challenges in meeting gaps in access, and in improving the nature, level and quality of services. In schools, the principal challenges are: to provide sufficient human and capital resources of the right type, both within the school and within its surrounding community; to ensure that these resources are dedicated to career guidance; and to make the best use of the resources that are available. Gaps in access are particularly evident in primary schools and in the vocational tracks of upper secondary school. Policy options include formally strengthening collaboration between all relevant stakeholders, making the acquisition of career management skills by students the focus of career education programmes, and improved accountability mechanisms.

A significant number of young people leave school early, without qualifications. They need programmes in the community to help them make transitions to the working world and to re-engage with further learning, and career guidance needs to be part of such programmes. Career guidance also needs to be a stronger part of programmes within the school designed to prevent early leaving.

There is generally a lack of career guidance provision for students in tertiary education, despite the significant cost of such studies to both participants and taxpayers. The range of career services that are offered within tertiary education needs to be broadened. Policy levers to ensure that a broader range of services is provided need to be strengthened. Options available to policy makers include the specification of goals for tertiary career services, and more explicitly linking public funding arrangements for tertiary education to the level and quality of career services.

Improving Career Guidance for Adults

The heterogeneous nature of the adult population presents a range of challenges to policymakers who are trying to improve career guidance services. Few easily accessible services are available for employed adults; few enterprises cater for the career development needs of their employees; fee-for-service provision that people can purchase privately is very limited; employers and trade unions have shown limited interest to date in providing career guidance even though they often recognise in principle the need for workforce development in order to improve competitiveness and equity. Despite these problems, new partnerships between employer organisations, education and training institutions, public employment services and other relevant organisations can lead to workplace and workforce career guidance provision, and career guidance should be an integral part of adult learning programmes.

Career guidance is seen as having a key role in preventing inflows into unemployment, particularly long-term unemployment. Public employment services (PES) in most countries have a lead role in such prevention. Yet career guidance services within the PES are undeveloped. Strong collaboration strategies, between the PES and private and community-based guidance services, and with local education and training institutions, can enable unemployed persons to make transitions to employment and to re-engage with learning.

Ageing populations and pension funding problems in many countries will require both later retirement ages and more flexible transitions to retirement. To date policymakers have been slow to mobilise career guidance services to support active ageing. Employers and worker representatives can promote and take initiatives in service delivery of third age guidance, using combinations of public and private partnerships.

Improving Access to Career Guidance Services

The demand for career guidance services exceeds its supply. More flexible delivery methods, including the use of ICT and of call centres, have great potential for extending access. If all citizens are to have access to career guidance, there is often a need to target career guidance services to at-risk groups. Actively involving vulnerable groups in designing, planning, implementing and monitoring career guidance policies and services for them greatly enhances the development of services that are relevant to their needs.

Improving the quality and relevance of career information materials to support universal access is an on-going challenge. There is often a lack of collaboration between different government ministries, agencies, and between national and regional levels of government in providing and sharing career information. Materials developed by the private sector are not subject to any agreed standards. In order to develop a coherent policy and strategy for the delivery of quality career information to citizens, national, regional and local mapping exercises of career guidance information provided through a range of media (such as newspapers and television) to a range of target groups (youth, employed, unemployed) is an essential starting point.

Improving the Systems that Support Career Guidance

Significant differences occur in the quality and types of career guidance services that are provided to citizens, both within and between countries, as the result of significant variations in the training of career guidance practitioners. The length of their initial training varies from three weeks to five years. Governments are very inactive in defining the content and process of initial training for career guidance practitioners, and in relating training content to the outcomes sought for public policy goals for education, training and employment. Stronger signals from ministries are required in order to bridge this gap.

There is little regular and systematic evaluation of the quality of career guidance provision in most countries. Service standards for provision do not exist or are present in some sectors but not in others. Quality frameworks, where they exist, tend to be voluntary rather than mandatory, and to operate as guidelines. Users of career guidance services have a key role to play in the design and evaluation of services.

The evidence base for policymaking for career guidance service provision is very weak. At present, few governments have in hand the data needed to provide an overall picture of career guidance provision, or of its effectiveness in meeting public policy objectives. Few government ministries are able to state precisely how much public money is being spent on career guidance services and how it is being spent. Information about private investment and expenditure in this field is not available. Collaboration among stakeholders (such as users, administrators, social partners and practitioners) at national level will help to identify relevant and useful data types and procedures for evaluating inputs, processes, outputs and outcomes for career guidance provision.

Career guidance objectives are weakly reflected in policies for education, training and employment in most countries. Given the inadequate evidence base for career guidance, this is not surprising. Furthermore career guidance provision is often a collection of disparate sub-systems within education, training, employment, community and private sectors, each with its own history, rationale and driving forces, rather than a coherent and integrated set of arrangements. The establishment of a national forum for guidance policy and systems development, which includes both government and key stakeholder representatives such as employers and trade unions, as well as the key organisations that deliver services, is an important step that governments can take to help to focus and develop policy agendas and to strengthen policy making.

Most of the cost of providing career guidance services is borne by taxpayers. The expansion in the extent, reach and variety of provision necessitated by a lifelong learning perspective signals new financial demands on and commitments from governments in an area that has tended to attract little individual and private investment. This demand on public resources may be moderated if more private investment can be stimulated.

1

INTRODUCTION

The context and purposes of this handbook

This handbook is a joint publication of the OECD and the European Commission[1]. It has been written to help policy makers in the member countries of both organisations to harness career guidance as a tool of public policy and to help them to develop, articulate and communicate effective policies for career guidance in education, training and employment. In the European context it is a response to on-going changes in education, training and employment policies arising from the Lisbon (2000) goals of making Europe the most competitive knowledge-based economy and society in the world by 2010, marked by social cohesion. Career guidance has become a particular focal point in such policy development: it is viewed as a key element of lifelong learning policies, of active employment policies, of social equity policies, and of strategies to attain the Lisbon goals.

Policy development in education and training within the European Union is being carried out by the member states, working in association with the European Commission's Directorate General for Education and Culture, through the Education and Training 2010 work programme. Given the relevance of career guidance for education, training and employment policies, the Commission established an Expert Group on Lifelong Guidance in December 2002 in which the OECD participates. This handbook is an initiative of the Expert Group.

The content of this handbook reflects the findings of recent international reviews of national career guidance policies. In 2001 the OECD commenced an international review to examine how the organisation, management and delivery of career guidance can assist countries in advancing some key public policy goals, and in particular those goals that arise from lifelong learning and active employment policies. The review involved 14 countries of which ten were members of the European Union, and was carried out in close co-operation with the European Commission. The OECD review was subsequently extended by the European Commission and the World Bank to include 19 other European countries. The results of these reviews are available in OECD (2004), Sultana (2004) and Watts and Fretwell (2004).

The handbook is intended to:

➤ Act as an easy reference guide that will enable policy makers in Europe and beyond to readily identify dimensions of policy that should be included in the process of decision making for guidance delivery in different settings in a lifelong learning framework;

➤ Provide good examples of policy to inform this work; and

➤ Identify appropriate methods for evaluating policies and their implementation.

Material for the handbook was prepared by Professor Ronald Sultana (Euro-Mediterranean Centre for Educational Research, University of Malta), and Professor Tony Watts (National Institute for Careers Education and Counselling, United Kingdom), with assistance from staff of the Directorate General,

---

[1] It is both an OECD publication and a European Commission staff working paper.

Education and Culture of the European Commission and Richard Sweet, OECD. The authors wish to express their thanks to the members of the European Commission's Expert Group on Lifelong Guidance for their helpful advice and support, and also to the individuals who commented on the drafts of particular sections.

Using this handbook

The main part of the handbook is divided into 14 policy themes, and these are organised in four sections: Improving career guidance for young people; Improving career guidance for adults; Improving access to career guidance; and Improving policies and systems for career guidance. For each of the 14 policy themes, the handbook provides:

➢ The key problems or issues that need to be considered (for example limited access to services; insufficient evidence on expenditure);

➢ A set of questions that policy makers need to ask in addressing these issues (for example: Which groups miss out on access? How much is spent on career guidance services?);

➢ Some options that policy makers can adopt to improve policies (for example setting targets for equity groups; evaluating benefits in relation to costs). The relevance of each these options will, of course, vary widely from country to country depending upon the level of development of national career guidance services; and

➢ Some examples of effective responses, drawn from the reviews conducted by the OECD and the European Commission.

The handbook concludes with an outline of some of the key features that policy makers should take into account in designing and implementing lifelong guidance systems. It also contains a number of technical annexes to support the material in the body of the handbook.

What is career guidance?

This handbook adopts the definition of career guidance that was used in recent international reviews conducted by the OECD, the European Commission and the World Bank:

> Career guidance refers to services and activities intended to assist individuals, of any age and at any point throughout their lives, to make educational, training and occupational choices and to manage their careers. Such services may be found in schools, universities and colleges, in training institutions, in public employment services, in the workplace, in the voluntary or community sector and in the private sector. The activities may take place on an individual or group basis, and may be face-to-face or at a distance (including help lines and web-based services). They include career information provision (in print, ICT-based and other forms), assessment and self-assessment tools, counseling interviews, career education programmes (to help individuals develop their self awareness, opportunity awareness, and career management skills), taster programmes (to sample options before choosing them), work search programmes, and transition services.

REFERENCES

OECD (2004), *Career Guidance and Public Policy: Bridging the Gap*, Paris.

Sultana, R.G. (2004), *Guidance Policies in the Knowledge Economy. Trends, Challenges and Responses Across Europe. A Cedefop Synthesis Report*, Cedefop Panorama series No. 85, Office for Official Publications of the European Commission, Luxembourg.

Watts, A.G. and D. H. Fretwell (2004), *Public Policies for Career Development. Case Studies and Emerging Issues for Designing Career Information and Guidance Systems in Developing and Transition Economies*, The World Bank, Washington.

2

CAREER EDUCATION AND GUIDANCE IN SCHOOLS

Policy Issues

In compulsory schooling

- The foundations of career self-management skills (for example decision making, self-awareness, self confidence) are laid at an early age. However career education and guidance in the primary school are limited or non-existent, and little systematic provision is made to explore the world of work.

- Young people need to make a smooth transition from primary school to the initial years of secondary education: the choices that they make at this point have major implications for later education and work options. Career guidance needs to be part of the process that helps them to make a smooth transition.

- Career education is increasingly present in the curriculum at the lower secondary school level, either as a separate subject or included in another subject. However it is included in widely differing ways, and at times these seem designed to suit the organisational needs of the school rather than the career development needs of the student. Often career education has little connection to the wider school curriculum.

- In lower secondary school personal career guidance frequently targets students at key decision-making points (when they are choosing subjects; prior to the end of compulsory schooling; at the transition to upper secondary level or to work). However often those who are targeted for personal interviews are not selected on the basis of well-defined need (for example low vocational maturity; readiness for decision making).

In upper secondary schooling

- It is often assumed that upper secondary students have made specific educational and career choices and that they do not need further support. This assumption is especially made for students in vocational education pathways. In many countries they receive significantly less career assistance than do students in general education pathways. This takes little account of the increasing flexibility that is included in upper secondary vocational education programmes, or of the wide range of career options and jobs that can flow from broadly designed vocational education and training.

- Within general education pathways career guidance staff often spend substantial time preparing students to choose and compete for tertiary education places. This can result in those not intending to enter tertiary education receiving little help. It can also lead to little account being taken of the occupational and labour market consequences of particular tertiary education choices.

Some issues that apply to all levels of schooling

- Those who provide career education and guidance in schools often lack specialised training.

- Those who provide career education and guidance in schools are often not career guidance specialists. They very often combine career guidance with other roles: teaching other school subjects; providing counselling and guidance for personal problems and study difficulties.

- The number of people employed to provide career education and guidance in schools is often not enough to meet student need and demand.

- Often services continue to be provided largely on an individual, face-to-face model. This reduces the capacity of the service to respond to the needs of all learners.

- Often career guidance staff do not have the resources that they need to do the job properly: a private space where students can be interviewed; a library of up-to-date career information; a computer; access to a telephone; secretarial assistance.

- Many school career guidance services have tenuous links with the world of work:

  ➤ Teaching staff know little about the labour market and what is involved in different types of jobs;

  ➤ Little contact exists with the public employment service;

  ➤ Students have very few or no opportunities to take part in work experience;

  ➤ Few employers are invited in to the school to talk to students;

  ➤ Parents have little involvement in the school's careers programme; and

  ➤ Careers fairs in which groups of employers come to the one location to provide information to students do not take place.

- Career education and guidance are often considered to be the sole responsibility of the specialist career guidance staff, rather than the joint responsibility of all members of the teaching staff.

- Few career guidance services have structured approaches aimed at helping students develop an entrepreneurial spirit and skills. They therefore tend to focus on guidance for paid employment, rather than for self-employment.

- School career guidance services are often not audited, and users have little opportunity to signal satisfaction or otherwise with the services provided. No data is collected on student, teacher, parent or employer satisfaction with the service.

Questions That Policies Need To Address

- How early should career education programmes commence in compulsory schooling? During primary school? During lower secondary school? How long should they continue? To the end of compulsory schooling, or into upper secondary education? Are there any special problems in ensuring that *all* students receive the assistance that they need? How can policies ensure that any such problems can be overcome? Where separate general and vocational education tracks exist in national school systems, how can policies ensure that students in each track receive the types of career education and guidance that they need?

- Should career education be a separate subject in the curriculum, or should it be integrated with other subjects? What are the implications of each option for the quality of the programme and for resources? If it is a separate subject, do links need to be made to other subjects? If it is not a separate subject, how should its delivery be co-ordinated? What should its objectives be? What should its content be? Who should teach it, and what training do they need?

- Within schools' overall careers programme, what should the balance be between career education lessons, personal interviews, and opportunities to explore and experience the world of work? Who should receive personal interviews, and when should these be held?

- What special provision, if any, needs to be made to assist disadvantaged students and potential early school leavers?

- What mix of personnel is required to deliver a comprehensive careers programme? Who should co-ordinate each school's overall careers programme? What balance is needed between teachers with specialist training who work on careers for only part of the time and full-time careers specialists? Should career guidance be a separate role within the school, or combined with other functions such as personal counselling? What external support is needed: from the public employment service; from community members; from employers; from alumni? What training programmes need to be put in place for these external personnel? Are special contracts or agreements needed at a national, regional or local level to support the role of external agencies?

- What special resources does each school need to ensure that its careers programme can be successfully implemented (dedicated office space, career information, teacher time, ICT)?

- Where school funding is decentralised, what policy levers are required in order to make sure that all students receive adequate career education and guidance, that programmes are of consistent quality across schools and regions, and that sufficient resources are devoted to career education and guidance?

- How should schools' careers programmes be monitored and evaluated? What types of data need to be collected at a central or national level to assist policy making?

Some Policy Options

- Conduct a national survey of schools' career education and guidance programmes in order to identify gaps in provision and the level and types of physical, human and financial resources that are used for these programmes.

CAREER GUIDANCE: A HANDBOOK FOR POLICY MAKERS – ISBN – 9264015191 © OECD/ EUROPEAN COMMUNITIES 2004

- Hold national, regional and local consultations with school principals, employers, parents and students on the needs for career education and guidance in schools. In these consultations seek views on issues such as the level of provision that is desirable, how student entitlements could be defined and implemented, and how consistency and quality can be ensured.

- Survey students' satisfaction with schools' career education and guidance programmes. In analysing the results of the survey, ensure that level of satisfaction is explored as a function of factors such as gender, school grade, and type of track or programme.

- Hold regular national regional and sectoral consultations with employers and labour market authorities to help ensure that labour market developments are integrated into school career education programmes.

- Survey students' use of and satisfaction with the career information materials that are used within schools. Use the outcomes of the survey to improve the quality of the material.

- Where gaps in provision exist, develop and evaluate pilot programmes as a basis for wider national programmes. Where personal career guidance is provided by non-specialists (for example by teachers on a part-time basis, or by general school counsellors or psychologists alongside personal counselling), develop and evaluate a pilot programme in which the service is provided by specialist career guidance staff.

- Develop guidelines for the physical space and resources that are needed to ensure an effective career education and guidance programme in a school.

- Create a national organisation, as a partnership between education authorities and employers, that can support schools in delivering work experience programmes, including ensuring employer support for work experience placements, and developing and monitoring guidelines for schools and employers to ensure the quality of programmes.

- Hold a national review of the initial and in-service training needs of the personnel who deliver career education and guidance in schools.

- Develop national guidelines on the types of outcomes that school career education and guidance programmes should be expected to achieve. Use these expected outcomes to monitor the quality and effectiveness of schools' programmes. Ensure that parents and local employers receive the results of evaluations carried out using these outcome measures.

- Conduct regular surveys of the educational and labour market destinations of school leavers. Ensure that schools are provided not only with aggregate national outcomes, but also the outcomes for their own students.

Examples of Effective Responses

- *The guidance-oriented school across primary and secondary education levels:* In Canada (Quebec), schools are being encouraged to develop the concept of the guidance-oriented school (*l'école orientante*). Personal and career planning is defined as one of five broad areas of learning throughout schooling. The aim is to provide support for students' identity development in primary school and guidance in career planning throughout secondary school. This is linked to ensuring that students understand the usefulness of their studies (in languages, mathematics, sciences and so on) and why they are studying them. To implement this concept, the number of qualified guidance specialists is being increased. In addition, the active involvement of all stakeholders is being promoted, first by encouraging discussion and collaboration between teachers and guidance staff, and then by developing partnerships with parents and the community. Schools are being permitted considerable flexibility in determining what a guidance-oriented school is, within the broad parameters provided.

- *Portfolio systems:* Some countries have developed strategies to help students integrate the knowledge, skills and attitudes concerning work that they have learnt from different teachers. These include the use of portfolios, where students record their career-related learning and experiences. Such a portfolio is referred to as a 'job passport' (Austria), an 'education log' (Denmark), and a 'career-choice passport' (Germany). It can help students to manage their own learning and see its relationship with their career plans.

- *Building bridges with the world of work:* A variety of 'work experience', 'work tasters', 'work shadowing' and 'work visit' initiatives may be organised to help students develop insights into the world of work and their own occupational orientations. In Germany, exploratory visits to enterprises are an integral part of career guidance, and generally involve an element of work experience. Companies value this form of contact with schools. Practical placements commonly last between one and three weeks, and teaching guides and support materials have been developed to support the placements and also the preparation and follow-up processes in schools. There are extensive health and safety provisions for legal and insurance-related reasons. In some cases, practical placements can also be spent in other European countries.

- *Career guidance as a cross-curricular responsibility of all school staff members:* In Finland, teachers and other partners have an operational description of their respective activities so that delivery of services is guaranteed. This ensures an improvement of the minimum-level service provision, while at the same time promoting institutional responsibility for career education and guidance at the school level.

- *Ensuring that career guidance personnel use people who know about the world of work:* Several countries are encouraging schools to develop partnerships in the provision of career guidance. Often such partnerships include calling on significant stakeholders – such as parents, alumni, and representatives from the business community, trade unions, and non-government organisations – to make an input into the career education programme. In some cases, the school devolves some of the responsibility for career guidance to an external agency, which it considers to be closer to the world of work. Such external provision should be seen as a complement to, rather than a substitute for, school-based provision. In such cases a formal co-operation contract is desirable (as in the German model, for instance).

3

CAREER GUIDANCE FOR YOUNG PEOPLE AT RISK

Policy Issues

- In some countries, services designed to quickly re-integrate early school leavers into learning and work are poorly developed. Where such re-integration services for young people who have left school early and who are at risk do exist, career guidance is not always part of them.

- A challenge for policy-makers is to make sure that career guidance is part of community-based services that are targeted at early school-leavers. These services need to be designed so that users can identify with the staff that work in them and can feel at home in them. A related challenge is to develop the capacity of communities where high levels of early school leaving occur to assist potential young school leavers to stay in school, or having left school, to help them to re-engage with learning.

- School career guidance services have often not been part of strategies to prevent early school-leaving, particularly by young people who are at risk of social exclusion. A challenge for policy-makers is to make sure that career guidance is part of schools' strategies to detect and assist young people who leave school early or without qualifications: to help them to find meaning in staying at school; or to have well planned exit strategies that will enable them to re-engage in learning, and successfully complete their secondary education and training. Where such programmes do not exist, a broader challenge is to work with educators to create them.

Questions That Policies Need To Address

- Where programmes do not exist in schools to detect and assist early school-leavers, what arguments can career guidance policy-makers and practitioners use to help create them? What career guidance should be provided to potential early school-leavers, and how? Should it be delivered as part of the curriculum or in addition to it? Should it be delivered by internal or external personnel or both? Should it include out of school experiential placements?

- What training and competencies do career guidance workers need to work with early school-leavers and at-risk youth? Do present career guidance workers have these competencies (for example referring users appropriately to other services and collaborating in cross-sectoral teams)? How should school and other education- and training-based career guidance personnel collaborate with out-of-school personnel such as youth workers, social workers, community workers and other adults to optimise the impact of both?

- Do community-based services for early school-leavers make adequate provision for career guidance as part of a wide range of individualised assistance?

▪ What career guidance is provided in second-chance learning programmes for early school leavers? How is guidance integrated into such programmes? What should its content be? How should it be delivered and by whom and when?

Some Policy Options

▪ Make career guidance for potential early school leavers a priority in the allocation of guidance resources to schools. Work with education system managers and school leaders to demonstrate the value of early intervention strategies to detect potential school drop-outs, and to show the role that educational and career guidance can play in such strategies.

▪ Improve the initial and in-service training of school principals, teachers and guidance workers to alert them to ways in which they can integrate career guidance into programmes to assist potential early school leavers.

▪ Make use of community outreach measures (delivered where young people congregate) and work through significant adults that are in daily contact with these young people to provide career guidance to at-risk young people.

▪ Ensure that training programmes for career guidance practitioners enable them to develop the skills to work with at-risk youth and school drop-outs, including skills in networking, collaboration with significant adults and agencies, referral and team work.

▪ Ensure that every early school-leaver has an individual action plan for further learning, work and other life goals.

▪ Ensure that schools undertake a follow-up of early school-leavers, providing career guidance assistance where required and where possible, for up to two years after the pupil has left school.

▪ Develop early intervention strategies working with and through families, meeting them in their homes, and organising assistance such as homework clubs.

Examples of Effective Responses

▪ *Integrated service delivery in Scandinavia:* The most successful policies for dealing with at-risk youth and school drop outs tend to be found in Scandinavia (although elements of the approach can be seen in other European countries). These policies have adopted an individualised approach in which personal, educational and occupational guidance are woven together with a range of other personal, educational and employment services: for example, help with health or housing, courses in basic literacy, job-seeking skills training, self-confidence building, learning-by-doing, or short periods of subsidised employment. This requires close co-operation between career guidance staff and a range of other workers. For school drop-outs, these initiatives combine early intervention, mutual obligation and individual action planning, with guidance being a major element of the process.

▪ *Proactive municipalities in Denmark:* Danish municipalities are legally obliged to make contact with young people who have dropped out of formal education on at least two occasions a year up to the age of 19. Some municipalities extend the system beyond this. In some cases this work is done by school guidance counsellors. In others, especially the larger municipalities, it is carried out by separate youth guidance counsellors. From the age of 18 such young people become entitled to limited income support, but only if they develop and implement action plans in consultation with the youth guidance service. The focus is on a mutual obligation approach designed to help them take up their rights to participate in education and training.

- *The Youthreach programme in Ireland:* This is targeted at unemployed youth, many of whom are early school-leavers. Individual programmes are located in a wide variety of settings: centres sponsored by local Vocational Education Committees; Community Training workshops funded by the Training and Employment Agency (FÁS); and Senior Traveller Training Centres. In the programme, the personal, social, educational and vocational problems experienced by many participants mean that advice, guidance and counselling often form an important part of the role of those who teach in the programme. Pilot programmes have been established to train them in guidance skills. In addition, a guidance service is provided to each programme by qualified personnel on a limited part-time basis: these include staff from the Training and Employment Agency.

4

CAREER SERVICES IN TERTIARY EDUCATION

Policy Issues

- There is little or no career guidance available for many students in tertiary education. Often, services are thin on the ground, with students not having access to the range of services they require to make informed educational and career decisions.

- There is a lack of trained personnel to meet tertiary students' career development and guidance needs.

- The focus of existing career services is frequently narrow, often concentrating on personal or study guidance. Little attention is paid to career development and choice, including helping students to develop career management and entrepreneurial skills and to consider taking up self-employment options.

- The specific career guidance needs of particular groups of students - including students in transition from study to employment, students who are dropping out from or changing their courses, mature students returning to study, distance learning students, and international students, for instance - are often not catered for.

Questions That Policies Need To Address

- Should tertiary institutions that are publicly funded be required to provide career services for students? If yes, then what level of service should be specified? Should this level of service be an entitlement?

- Should the quality of career services, and the skills and qualifications of the staff providing these services, be a part of the general assessment of the quality of tertiary institutions?

- What central careers services are needed within a tertiary education institution? How should such services relate to the roles of teaching staff and to the content of the academic curriculum (in particular where career development and work-based learning are required as part of academic courses)?

- How should tertiary careers services link with external career guidance and employment services, as well as with employers, to ensure that career information and career guidance are appropriate, up-to-date and informed by accurate labour market information?

- How should career guidance and development be integrated more closely into teaching and learning programmes across faculties and departments?

CAREER GUIDANCE: A HANDBOOK FOR POLICY MAKERS – ISBN – 9264015191 © OECD/ EUROPEAN COMMUNITIES 2004

- How should career self management and career development courses within the curriculum be promoted, and profiling and portfolio systems developed?

- What evidence about outcomes (for example on graduate destinations, non-completion rates and destinations of non-completers, annual costs of non-completion) should be collected? How can this information be used to improve career services for current students and to improve the enrolment decisions of prospective students?

- How should students, employers, and other stakeholders be involved in the development and delivery of more effective career services?

- What policy levers and resource incentives can be used to stimulate and influence the development of career services in tertiary education, given the high degree of autonomy that this sector has had traditionally?

- How are the career guidance needs of various target groups in tertiary education (for example adult learners, persons with disabilities, persons with very limited financial support, foreign students, drop-outs) catered for?

Some Policy Options

- Establish a national review of career services in tertiary education, and ensure that its results are widely distributed and publicised in the media.

- As part of such a review, develop a questionnaire on tertiary career services that can be used both for national and institutional service audits. Ensure that students, both present and past, are asked for their opinions, as well as other stakeholders such as employers, faculty members and families. In administering and analysing such a questionnaire, target specific groups of students such as adult learners, students in transition, international students, the disadvantaged and the disabled.

- Review the qualifications of career service staff in tertiary education and propose and implement required changes in their initial and continuing training and training for the management of such services.

- Link tertiary education career services to national tertiary education funding arrangements: for example by requiring them to be included as part of performance targets, strategic planning, or quality assurance arrangements.

- Ensure that consistent national data is collected on the labour market and educational outcomes of tertiary education graduates (for example industry and occupation of employment, earnings, unemployment rates, further studies undertaken). Ensure that such data is widely distributed to present and prospective students, to employers, and to tertiary education administrators and academic staff.

- Investigate course non-completion rates in tertiary institutions, the actual costs associated with non-completion, and the cost-benefit ratio of providing career guidance services prior to course entry and during course participation.

- Establish a national network between tertiary education career services and other career guidance providers and stakeholders, particularly labour market-based career guidance services, to ensure that students are provided with adequate labour market information.

- Promote a diversified approach to the provision of career guidance services in tertiary education taking into account the needs of various target groups with targeted funding as an incentive.

- Provide seed funding for innovation and development of career services in tertiary education.

Examples of Effective Responses

- *The Careers Advisory Service at Trinity College Dublin* (http://www.tcd.ie/Careers/) provides a wide range of services to students, graduates, academic staff and employers. In addition to personal advice, students have access to a comprehensive careers library and to a wide range of on-line resource materials, which are also available elsewhere on campus and off-campus.

- The service organises careers days that enable students to make contact with employers to discuss post-graduation employment. It provides students with access to job vacancies, and helps to arrange internships, work experience and vacation employment. Regular seminars are held throughout the year on job-seeking skills, including video rehearsal of interview skills. Students can have access to psychological testing to assist their career decision-making. The service arranges opportunities for students to be mentored by recent young graduates for short periods in order to better prepare themselves for post-graduation employment. A personal development programme is run within a number of the university's departments to help develop employability skills.

- Graduates of Trinity College are able to use the service for personal advice (with a charge to those in employment), for help with job placement, and to use the careers library. Employers are provided with access to students for recruitment purposes, and can post vacancies with the service and on its website. A range of company directories are available in the service, employers are regularly surveyed on the qualities that they require in graduates, and graduates are surveyed six months after graduation to determine their destinations.

- Specified academic staff in each faculty or department is responsible for liaising with the Careers Advisory Service. The service works actively with academic staff to ensure that they refer students appropriately to the service. Academic staff have close involvement with the student personal development programme, which is a formal part of the academic curriculum.

5

CAREER GUIDANCE FOR UNEMPLOYED ADULTS

Policy Issues

- The immediate needs of many job seekers require comprehensive career guidance so that they can access a range of support services to increase their employability. These include training, retraining, and work experience, in addition to ongoing help with job search and job placement. A key policy challenge is to ensure that they receive such support services.

- Preventing inflows into unemployment, particularly into long-term unemployment, preventing skill mismatches, encouraging regional labour mobility, and developing employability skills are key parts of national, European and international employment strategies. Public employment services (PES) in most countries have a lead role in such strategies. Yet career guidance services within the PES are underdeveloped, and are not systematically linked to the implementation of these goals.

- Within most PES, those who provide career guidance for the unemployed often have to undertake other tasks as well: for example, policing benefit entitlements; information-giving; and job placement. This reduces the priority that they can give to career guidance. It can also lead to conflicts of interest between competing priorities of placement targets and career guidance.

- Career guidance personnel in the PES tend to have limited specialised training. Their training often targets the development of organisational and administrative skills rather than of career guidance competencies.

- Many groups of unemployed adults have quite different characteristics and problems (for example older workers, women returning to work after child rearing, ethnic minorities and people with disabilities). Yet often the career guidance available to them does not cater for their distinctive needs.

- Community-based career guidance services are often closer to the needs of citizens, and therefore more effective in reaching targeted groups of adults. A policy challenge here is how far to stimulate outsourcing of these services, while at the same time ensuring quality provision in line with nationally accepted standards and objectives.

- In providing career guidance services to unemployed adults, despite significant progress in modernising the PES in many countries, insufficient use is made of more cost-effective delivery methods such as outreach-working through related professionals, one-stop shops, self-service, ICT, or services of differing intensity to reflect different levels of need.

Questions That Policies Need To Address

- To what extent is career guidance provided within the PES undertaking a proactive role to help improve employability, increase labour flexibility, and reduce levels of long-term unemployment? Does the career guidance provided by the PES have the capacity and flexibility to reach and re-motivate unemployed individuals to re-engage with learning and work? To what extent is career guidance provided by the PES capable of outreach to geographically and economically disadvantaged communities? Is a different but related careers service required?

- To what extent is the PES networking and in partnership with the relevant actors in the field of guidance so that they can widen their range of services to the unemployed, and permit localised and decentralised delivery of careers guidance?

- What are the views of target groups of the unemployed on the career guidance services provided to them by the PES and other organisations?

- To what extent are the users of the PES, and of other organisations providing career guidance to the unemployed, involved in the design and evaluation of the services provided to them?

- What are the distinctive career guidance needs of different groups of unemployed adults? To what extent are these needs being met by current provision? How can services be organised so that such a range of needs is more effectively catered for?

- Is career guidance an integral part of activation measures designed to increase the capacities and competencies of unemployed people at risk of social exclusion?

- How can career guidance for unemployed adults provided by the PES be complemented by services provided by voluntary and community-based organisations, by the social partners, and private, for-profit services?

- How can standards of career guidance services be maintained where they are provided to unemployed adults by a wide range of organisations (government, voluntary, private)?

- How can public employment services help unemployed adults to quickly get into work, but also address their longer-term career development needs?

- How can public employment services support the lifelong learning needs of unemployed adults?

- Is the PES a market leader for employment services, including career information services, on the Internet?

- How can ICT be harnessed to improve service delivery in cost-effective ways, and to encourage self-service access to information? What type of assistance is required by which type of user of the information systems provided?

- How can the PES guarantee the quality, content and relevance of the career information provided through its services?

- How is the European and international dimension of the labour market presented to jobseekers?

CAREER GUIDANCE: A HANDBOOK FOR POLICY MAKERS – ISBN – 9264015191 © OECD/ EUROPEAN COMMUNITIES 2004

Some Policy Options

- Review current national and international employment policies, strategies and guidelines. Consider where career guidance best fits within the employment activation and unemployment prevention measures proposed.

- Ensure that the immediate needs of jobseekers are addressed by providing them with comprehensive career guidance support so that they can access a job or other employability measure, or learning opportunities such as training and retraining, combined where appropriate with ongoing job search assistance.

- Draw up a strategy for co-operative relationships between the PES and education and training institutions, community, voluntary and private career guidance agencies to provide appropriate career guidance services to the unemployed.

- Ensure that the PES recruits trained career guidance staff, and that it has a well-developed in-service training strategy for those that have been recruited in the past without specific guidance competencies. Maintain the knowledge and skills of career guidance staff in a rapidly changing labour market.

- Undertake country peer reviews of career guidance services for the unemployed and publicise the results widely.

- Review existing provision for careers guidance services for the unemployed using, for example, the Guidelines for Good Practice in Employment Counselling and Guidance (1998) as benchmarks.

- Develop strategies to actively involve vulnerable groups in the design, planning, implementation and monitoring of policies and services for career guidance.

- Establish and update local labour market data systems and make sure that these are used by those who provide career guidance for the unemployed.

- Consider separating career guidance functions from other roles performed by staff in the PES.

- Where a decision is made to retain integrated provision, ensure that distinctive attention is given to career guidance.

- Stimulate community-based and private for-profit career guidance services: for example by outsourcing and contracting-out.

- Establish quality criteria for career guidance services aimed at unemployed adults.

- Develop user feedback mechanisms to ensure that unemployed adults' career guidance needs are being met.

- Ensure that career guidance is an integral part of adult learning programmes in publicly funded education and training institutions.

Examples of Effective Responses

- *Catering for the differentiated needs of unemployed adults through tiered services:* Tiered services can free up time and resources for guidance. In the public employment services in Austria, and to a lesser extent in Finland, Germany, the Netherlands, Portugal, and the United Kingdom, three levels or tiers of service tend to be distinguished:

  ➢ At the first level, people can access printed, audio-visual or on-line information in a self-service mode, without the need for staff to assist them.

  ➢ A second tier of service consists of relatively brief personal interviews.

  ➢ A third tier of service provides personal guidance to those who are perceived to need it and/or feel they can benefit from it. This can range from group help to in-depth personal interviews, and can include job clubs, and sessions that help users to recover self-confidence and motivation and to develop their employability skills.

- *Improving the training of staff offering career guidance in public employment services:* In Ireland, nearly eight in ten of the employment service staff who provide career guidance have had some form of guidance training. They can undertake a part-time university course in adult guidance over a twelve-month period, with their tuition fees and release time for course attendance being paid for, and with salary increments for those who successfully complete the course. A goal has been set to increase the number of staff who will possess such qualifications.

- *Harnessing ICT to develop self-service approaches to guidance:* In the Netherlands, a new web site has been developed (https://www.werk.nl/) which includes diagnostic instruments (based on interests), data on occupations (including labour-market trends and salary data), information on education and training opportunities, and access to a web version of the database of job vacancies. There are also plans to develop a user-support centre, to be accessible by telephone, e-mail, fax and post. In Belgium (Flanders), the public employment service (VDAB) has introduced a system of universal services based on increasing the use of instruments that allow self-assessment and self-steering by people looking for work, and to change their employment. MY VDAB is a further step in the evolution of a generation of tools that support user independence and the use of an electronic portfolio. It integrates existing instruments, such as information on vacancies, curricula vitae, and training possibilities, and brings them on line so that people can manage their own profile and can compare the information they have about themselves with other data-sets. VDAB also has a '*clientvolgsysteem*', which makes it possible to follow up users in the different stages of the pathways they embark upon. Clients are offered a manual to support them in exploiting the many services available on-line.

- *Community-based guidance services:* In Luxembourg, local action projects run by voluntary and not-for-profit organisations include the Full Employment Network (*Réseau Objectif Plein Emploi*), a programme for women who are victims of domestic violence (the *Femmes en Détresse* project), and local and regional development projects. In Canada, it is estimated that there are over 10,000 community-based organisations delivering career development services. Many are small, with perhaps five to seven full-time-equivalent staff; though some are much larger, with as many as 100 or 200 employees over a variety of locations. Some of these organisations focus on career development activities such as information services, career guidance and job-search workshops. Others have a wider range of functions, including various forms of learning programmes and community work. Some programmes, such as literacy programmes, may include career development elements, so enabling them to adopt more holistic approaches to the needs of their users.

REFERENCE

European Foundation for the Improvement of Living and Working Conditions (1998), Guidelines for Good Practice in Employment Counselling and Guidance, http://www.eurofound.eu.int/publications/files/EF9834EN.pdf

6

CAREER GUIDANCE FOR EMPLOYED ADULTS

Policy Issues

- Employed adults need access to career guidance for career development within their company, for career development outside it in similar work, or to retrain in new skills so that they can move into different types of jobs. Yet very few career guidance services are available for employed adults. Employed adults are less likely to access career guidance services than are unemployed adults. Services for employed adults are underdeveloped in the public, voluntary and private sectors in most countries. To support lifelong learning and active employment policies, more career guidance services need to be available for the employed.

- Few enterprises provide career development services for their employees. The services that are available tend to be confined to larger organisations. They are mostly provided for managerial and professional staff, not for the full range of employees. And they are largely targeted at career development within the enterprise, with little attention to career opportunities outside of the enterprise. Very few employer organisations attempt to provide such services that are independent of the interests of particular enterprises: for example on a fee for service basis.

- Trade unions have shown limited interest in the development of career guidance services for their members. Where they offer such services themselves, these tend to be delivered by non-specialised personnel and focus on access to training rather than wider career development.

- Public employment services tend to narrowly target the unemployed, rather than employed adults who wish to re-engage in learning or to develop their careers.

- Where private employment services exist, they focus on job brokerage and head hunting, and on outplacement for redundant workers. A few services offer personal career guidance to executives. Only rarely do they offer guidance for career development to a broad range of users.

- In nearly all countries there is a very limited private market for career guidance. This limits access to services by employed adults who could afford to pay.

Questions That Policies Need To Address

- To what extent do national policies support the development of services that can meet the full range of employed adults' career development needs? What career guidance services are available to employed adults, and who provides them?

- How can companies be encouraged to offer career guidance to their employees, and to support their career development?

- How can small and medium-sized enterprises be supported in developing career guidance services for their employees?

- How can companies, trade unions, professional bodies, employers' organisations, educational institutions, public and private employment services, and community-based organisations collaborate in delivering career guidance effectively to adults?

- How can a larger private market for career guidance be stimulated?

Some Policy Options

- Examine the sectoral, regional and local implications for career guidance of national and international policies for workforce development and lifelong learning - for example the "Framework of actions for the lifelong development of competencies and qualifications" (2002) agreed by the European social partners.

- Seek ways to widen the role of the PES in providing career guidance to employed adults.

- Stimulate career guidance in companies by introducing incentives: for example making career guidance an allowable expenditure under training levy schemes; or introducing schemes that give public recognition to enterprises that provide exemplary programmes.

- Encourage and promote partnerships between employer organisations, education and training institutions, public employment services and other relevant organisations to provide workplace guidance services, particularly for smaller enterprises.

- Encourage and offer support to professional bodies and trade unions to provide quality career guidance services to their members.

- Ensure that policies for continuing training of the workforce stress the importance of career guidance for employees as a way to ensure efficient investment in training.

- Ensure that career guidance is part of employee training programmes funded through government training levies on employers.

- Ensure that career guidance for employees features on the negotiating table in the collective bargaining of the social partners at national and sector levels.

- Provide a good model for the non-state sector by introducing policies that support the career development of employees in the public sector.

- Encourage the creation of larger private markets for career guidance: for example through the use of contracting out and guidance vouchers to encourage a wider range of fee for service private providers.

- Extend services that are already available in the adult and continuing education sectors to employed adults.

- Encourage the development of national telephone help lines for information and advice on lifelong learning.

- Improve the continued employment chances of adults through including accreditation and validation of prior learning programmes within career guidance services.

- Encourage the development of quality Internet career guidance services for adult workers to help them with career development issues.

- Ensure that the European and international dimension of the labour market is presented to job seekers and workers seeking career change, including (in Europe) through the use of EURES, the European PES network[2].

- Ensure that career guidance is an integral part of adult learning programmes in publicly funded education and training institutions.

Examples of Effective Responses

- *Career guidance in public employment services:* Some PESs indicate that they cater for the guidance needs of employed adults by organising the flow of users through the service in a way that reduces its association with the stigma of unemployment and welfare benefit queues. Norway is an example. Its public employment service centres are being redesigned to include state-of-the-art amenities that are attractive and accessible. Welfare-claimant services operate discreetly behind screens at the back. Facilities include printed vacancy information, word-processing for writing job applications and curricula vitae, free telephones for contacting employers, and some limited staff support. In addition, a range of self-help tools has been developed, many of them web-based. These include: an interests inventory; a career choice programme which offers self-assessments of interests, work values and skills, plus an occupational matching facility and help with job-seeking; and a career learning programme addressed mainly to higher education graduates.

- *Company-based career guidance services:* In the Netherlands, a few large employers have established mobility centres for their employees. These centres are often staffed by human resource development specialists, who are supported by external consultants. They provide training needs assessments. The centres are concerned mainly with internal movement within the company, but may also enable employees to explore opportunities in the external labour market, depending on whether the company is prepared to support this or not. In the United Kingdom, some employers are experimenting with combinations of call centres, electronic support and trained career advisers employed by the business.

- *Government incentives for the development of company-based guidance services:* Career guidance can be included as allowable expenditure against training levies. In the Netherlands, some sectors of employment have developed their own training schemes, based on training levy funds from employers and employees. These are particularly important for small and medium sized enterprises, which often lack their own training arrangements. The schemes may include access to some limited sector-specific career guidance from training officers. Another form of government incentive is voluntary quality-mark schemes. In the Netherlands and the United Kingdom, a government-

---

[2] http://europa.eu/int/eures/index.jsp

subsidised Investors in People programme provides a quality-mark to companies that adopt good human resource development practices. In the United Kingdom the matrix standard can award accreditation to organisations which provide information, advice and guidance on learning and work for their staff. In the Netherlands, this includes encouragement for companies to use careers advisers to support their development review systems.

- *Career guidance services and trade unions:* Unions may negotiate for the provision of guidance services with employers in the process of collective bargaining. They may also themselves provide guidance. In Denmark, Norway and the United Kingdom, some unions have run courses to train their shop stewards to act as 'educational ambassadors' or 'learning representatives' in encouraging their members (especially those with limited or no qualifications) to access education and training. This programme is extensive in the United Kingdom and receives strong support both from government and from the trade union movement (http://www.learningservices.org.uk/).

- *Career guidance services and accreditation of prior learning:* Career guidance services are often involved in the accreditation of prior learning, as this facilitates both the career development and the career mobility of workers. In Portugal, a National System of Recognising, Validating and Certifying Prior Learning (RVCC) is being implemented through a network of centres. Adults, whether employed or unemployed, are offered a three-tiered service, namely information, counselling, and complementary training, including the accreditation of competencies. Careers guidance providers and public and private enterprises refer people to the centres. By 2006, the network is expected to consist of 84 RVCC centres, distributed throughout the country in relation to density of population and school level.

REFERENCE

European Trade Union Confederation, Union of Industrial and Employers' Confederations of Europe, European Centre of Enterprises with Public Participation and of Enterprises of General Economic Interest (2002), *Framework of Actions for the Lifelong Development of Competencies and Qualifications* http://www.etuc.org/en/index.cfm?target=/en/dossiers/colbargain/lll.cfm.

7

CAREER GUIDANCE FOR OLDER ADULTS

Policy Issues

- Ageing populations in many OECD and European countries will require both later retirement ages and more flexible transitions to retirement. But policy-makers have been slow to mobilise career guidance services in order to support active ageing.

- Older adults need specialised information and advice to support active ageing: more fulfilling leisure; voluntary work; and activities to keep themselves mentally and physically fit. Yet career guidance services currently provide little help with this stage of people's lives.

- Flexible transitions between full-time work and full-time retirement (mixing full-time work, part-time work, voluntary work and periods of inactivity) will require much closer harmonisation of career planning and financial planning. This issue needs to be addressed by policy-makers.

- There are few examples of effective responses to the challenge of providing career guidance services to older adults. No country seems yet to have developed a systematic approach in this area.

Questions That Policies Need To Address

- What implications do lifelong learning and active ageing policies have for the provision of career guidance for older adults?

- Given present demographic projections, what is future demand for third-age career guidance likely to be?

- How can career guidance help to encourage people to create more flexible pathways between full-time work and full-time retirement (for example blending part-time work, voluntary work and short periods of full-time work with leisure)?

- Given the complex interactions that exist between taxation, retirement income, pension arrangements and working hours and employment contracts, how can a closer integration between career guidance and financial planning be created for older adults? How should such integrated services be funded?

- What special training is needed by career guidance staff working in this area?

- Which institutions, associations and groups are likely to be interested in developing and to be competent to develop third-age career guidance services? How can governments work in partnership with them?

Some Policy Options

- Ensure that career guidance is an integral part of adult learning programmes in publicly funded education and training institutions.

- Draw on available evidence, or commission research on, the correlation between active ageing and health.

- Develop links with investment and retirement funds to discuss links between financial planning, career planning and flexible transitions to retirement.

- Stimulate career guidance provision for older adults by outsourcing to associations that work closely with them.

- Adopt innovative approaches to service delivery, based around ICT and telephone technology, in order to cater for unmet needs.

- Explore how the role of the public employment services might be expanded to better cater for the career guidance needs of older adults.

- Encourage enterprise and community based initiatives to reverse the trend to early exit and long-term unemployment among older workers.

- Support the potential role of industry in preparing older employees for active retirement.

- Encourage employers to make career guidance a part of retraining and work redesign strategies to retain older workers for longer periods.

Examples of Effective Responses

- *Third-age career guidance projects:* In Denmark, a number of third-age career guidance projects have been implemented. One was funded by the Danish trade union of engineers and targeted senior engineers in Frederiksborg County. Another was funded by the Ministry of Finance.

- *Supporting work-force re-entry:* In Western Australia, the Profit from Experience Programme, funded by the State's Department of Training and accessed through community-based centres, supports mature-age people to re-enter the workforce.

8

EXPANDING ACCESS TO CAREER GUIDANCE

Policy Issues

- The demand for career guidance exceeds the supply, and many people do not have access to it. It is delivered in too limited a range of locations, ways, times of the day or week, or points in the life cycle. Employed adults, tertiary students, mothers with young children, women returning to work, older adults, people with disabilities, remote communities, and a range of disadvantaged groups are among those whose needs are not adequately catered for.

- The expensive and labour-intensive model of face-to-face interviewing is still widely used in career guidance. More cost-effective delivery methods could increase access to services for greater numbers of clients. These methods include self-service approaches and one-stop-shops; systematic use of networks of career mentors; embedding career education programmes in the school and tertiary education curriculum; group career guidance; and new technologies, including ICT and call centres.

- Career guidance is not widely available in workplace settings or in sites such as leisure centres, small communities, shopping malls, public libraries, citizen advice centres, community centres, and homes. Little of it is available outside of the standard opening hours of educational institutions and government offices. Peripatetic services, outreach services and shift work are not widely used to deliver career guidance.

- Public provision of career guidance services needs to be supplemented by private, enterprise-based and community-based provision. A policy challenge here is to find ways of stimulating such involvement through partnerships and outsourcing.

Questions That Policies Need To Address

- In which sectors and in which communities are demands for career guidance services clearly not being met? How do we know?

- If there is a legal entitlement to career guidance, how is this right promoted so that individuals are encouraged to exercise it?

- What is the optimum mix between public, private and community-based provision that will ensure improved coverage of career guidance needs?

- What strategies can be developed to support non-formal and informal career guidance (for example, through supplying training and information materials to underpin career guidance in community-based and other settings)?

- What investments in training, support, and communications infrastructure need to be made in order to develop ICT-based service delivery?

- What alternative strategies can be mobilised in countries and regions where the communications infrastructure is still underdeveloped? What use could be made of television, newspaper inserts, billboards, and peripatetic services?

- What kind of resources – including interest inventories, career navigation tools and checklists, job information videos, and so on – have been or could be developed in order to support a self-service approach to career guidance? Are these readily available via the internet and or on CD-ROM technology? What sorts of changes to staffing structures, as well as training and staff development initiatives, are needed to support self-service approaches?

- How can career guidance services be organised so that they are more readily accessible: out of standard office hours; in a self-service mode; in community-based resource centres? Do these changes involve re-negotiating staff working conditions?

Some Policy Options

- Undertake national, regional and local mapping of career guidance provided through a range of media (such as newspapers and TV) to a range of target groups (youth, employed, unemployed) in order to optimise future policy options.

- Stimulate career guidance in the private and voluntary sectors by developing partnerships with providers in the public sector, and through outsourcing.

- Promote the use of telephone help lines and e-mail-based services for career guidance to overcome geographical disadvantage and to allow access out of standard office hours.

- Include provisions for shift work in career guidance staff employment contracts.

- Ensure that the resources are available to support peripatetic and community-based delivery (cars; mobile phones; laptops; printed career information).

- Extend the opening times of public employment career guidance services, so that they are more readily accessible to employed people.

- Provide seed money and venture funding to support the development of ICT-based, self-service forms of career guidance delivery.

- Develop, adapt or adopt ICT-based career guidance programmes, and make them readily available via the internet and CD-ROM.

- Develop innovative ways of mixing on-line with off-line services to ensure customised delivery that meets the distinctive needs of clients.

- Develop quality assurance mechanisms to ensure that the extension of career guidance services and products takes place within a quality assurance framework.

- Develop and promote the use of user-screening processes to identify clients who are in need of the most intensive and expensive types of services, and match services to them in a cost-effective way.

- Provide career guidance in the sites and public spaces where citizens congregate, through Internet points and community information centres.

- Contract some career guidance services out to community groups.

- Ensure that the curricula of initial and in-service training programmes for career guidance personnel teach the skills required for effective use of ICT, both by themselves and by clients.

- Develop differentiated career guidance staffing and qualifications structures, with support staff working alongside more highly qualified staff in delivering services (for example, in providing help with information searches).

Examples of Effective Responses

- *Providing career guidance through call-centre technology:* The core of the *learndirect* service in the United Kingdom is built around call-centre technology. There are two call-centres in England, one for Northern Ireland, and smaller centres in Scotland and Wales. The *learndirect* initiative is funded through the University for Industry, and aspires to offer free and impartial advice that can assist adults to access further education and training opportunities. Such information includes, for instance, availability of funding for learning, and of childcare facilities to support parents with young children. To be as accessible as possible, the call-centre help-lines are open all year round till ten in the evening. Over five million people called *learndirect* in its first five years of operation. There are three tiers of staff: 'Information Advisers' handle basic information inquiries; 'Learning Advisers' handle the inquiries of those who need more than basic information; 'Lifelong Learning Advisers' deal with more complex requests. All staff levels receive special training, and all have access to an online database of information on some 600,000 education and training courses, at all levels, as well as to a wide variety of other printed information. The online database can be accessed directly at http://www.learndirect.co.uk/, and is updated monthly. An online diagnostic package can be used to assess interests and preferences as part of the web site. There were over 10 million hits on the site in its first years of operation.

- *Private-sector ICT-based guidance:* In 1999 *Helsingin Sanomat*, the newspaper with the widest circulation in Finland, made career services available to all citizens on the Internet. The newspaper's website (http://www.oikotie.fi) offers those who access it a multitude of career planning and job search tools and services. All services, including online self-assessment exercises, e-mail guidance, a Curriculum Vitae Wizard, and an option to forward applications to employers online, are free of charge.

- *Mobile centres:* Some countries have made innovative use of mobile, peripatetic guidance teams to cover communities that are hard to reach, or because there are not enough resources to cover demand. Latvia has so far managed to establish Professional Career Guidance Centres in only 19 of its 26 regions. But its mobile teams cater for the needs of the other seven.

9

CAREER GUIDANCE FOR DISADVANTAGED GROUPS

Policy Issues

- Few countries have yet found an effective balance between comprehensive career guidance services, available equally to all, and targeted provision that gives special priority to particular disadvantaged groups that have specific needs.

- The full potential of career guidance to help identify and re-motivate under-achieving students in order to significantly lower drop-out rates, or to attract disaffected youth back into education and training, has not yet been fully harnessed.

- Many of the marginalised and disadvantaged groups targeted by career guidance services tend to be the most reluctant to use services that are administered in a formal institutional context. The policy challenge here is to reach out to these groups, to work with them on their own terms and in contexts that are less formal and more familiar to them.

- Education and training programmes designed for at-risk groups need to include strong career guidance elements to promote re-engagement with learning and course completion, and to secure successful transition to sustainable employment.

Questions That Policies Need To Address

- How effectively is career guidance integrated into policies and programmes designed to address national equity goals? For example those that address: the integration of immigrants and refugees into employment and training; gender equity in the labour market; and equity in all levels of educational participation, completion and outcomes?

- What data exist on the use of career guidance services by disadvantaged and at-risk groups and their satisfaction with such services? Are career guidance services required to collect and analyse such data?

- Have alternative forms of career guidance service delivery been developed to overcome the reluctance of some disadvantaged groups to use the services offered by formal institutions?

- What resources exist in the community which are close to the target groups? Can these be mobilised (for example through out-sourcing) to provide career guidance services in a manner that is more likely to be accepted by such groups?

- Do training programmes for career guidance staff pay attention to the distinctive needs of different target groups, and equip them with the knowledge, skills and attitudes to work effectively with these groups?

- What steps are being taken to ensure that the career guidance approaches used with at-risk groups are not culturally biased?

Some Policy Options

- Develop strategies to actively involve vulnerable groups in designing, planning, implementing and monitoring career guidance policies and services.

- Given that many disadvantaged groups mainly seek work locally, establish and update local labour market information systems.

- Review existing career guidance services for vulnerable groups: for example using the *Guidelines for Good Practice in Employment Counselling and Guidance* (1998) as benchmarks.

- Subcontract career guidance services to agencies that are experienced in working with specific disadvantaged groups, and support such organisations through training and resourcing.

- Build up the capacity of vulnerable groups to help themselves to provide career guidance: for example by training respected adults within such groups to act as learning and guidance facilitators.

- Ensure that career guidance workers have the training required to work through and collaborate effectively with different at-risk groups. Ensure that such training involves inter-cultural awareness.

- Establish clear criteria for targeting at-risk groups.

- Make sure that data on the use of career guidance services by disadvantaged groups, and their satisfaction with these services, is collected and analysed.

- Evaluate how career guidance helps to advance social equity and social inclusion policy goals.

Examples of Effective Responses

- *Local centres:* In Greece, Information and Counselling Centres for Women's Employment and Social Integration have been set up, with the support of European Union funding, by the Research Centre for Gender Equality (KETHI). The centres offer services specifically to women, both to those who are unemployed, and to those who are in vulnerable employment sectors and wish to change jobs. The centres have developed a tool for identifying women's needs. Named '*To tychero Trifylli*' ('the Lucky Clover'), and adapted from a tool used by French counselling centres, it explores the needs of women in three basic categories: personal development, knowledge of the professional sector, and methods of seeking work.

- *Action projects:* In Luxembourg, local action projects run by voluntary and not-for-profit organisations include the Full Employment Network (*Reseau Objectif Plein Emploi*), a programme for women who are victims of domestic violence (the *Femmes en détresse* project) and local and regional development projects. Such projects are financed from a range of sources.

REFERENCE

European Foundation for the Improvement of Living and Working Conditions (1998), Guidelines for Good Practice in Employment Counselling and Guidance, http://www.eurofound.eu.int/publications/files/EF9834EN.pdf

IMPROVING CAREER INFORMATION

Policy Issues

- There is a major gap between the collection of labour-market information and its transformation into usable learning material for career guidance.

- Some industries face skill shortages. Often young people and adults know very little about these shortages.

- Up-dating of career information is a major challenge, particularly in countries with relatively low GDP per capita.

- In some countries career information is not comprehensive and is of poor quality. This seriously hinds the possibility of citizens making well informed and satisfying career decisions.

- There is often a lack of collaboration between different government agencies, and in particular between education and labour portfolios, and between different levels of government - and in particular between national and regional governments - in providing and sharing career information. This leads to costly overlap, fragmentation, and lack of transparency and comprehensiveness.

- The lack of such collaboration results in a failure to integrate information on the content of jobs, information on education and training options and pathways, and information on labour market supply and demand. A closely related problem is the failure to integrate career information with self-assessment tools, career planning tools and job search tools.

- Experience is a powerful way of learning, and of seeing the personal significance of things that have been learned by reading or in the classroom. People who are known and trusted are other powerful sources of information that is converted into personal action. However often career information systems fail to systematically allow people to experience work or new educational settings, and they make little use of networks of community members such as employers or the alumni of educational institutions.

- A lot of career information is produced by the private sector. However few countries have either mandated standards or voluntary guidelines for the collection, production and dissemination of career information by the public and private sectors.

- Governments make too little use of the expertise of the private sector in marketing, in publishing and in the media when they produce and disseminate career information products. As a result a lot of career information is uninteresting to look at, poorly designed, and does not reach the right targets.

- Very little career information is designed using research on client needs for different types of career information, on their preferences for different ways of delivering it, or on their satisfaction with existing career information products.

- ICT- and web-based career information systems are often nothing more than electronic versions of print-based material. This fails to make use of the potential of ICT-based systems to provide career information in far more interesting, flexible and intuitive ways.

- Increasingly, governments are developing career information largely in electronic form. However those who do not have ready access to ICT or who do not have the skills or confidence to use it are disadvantaged by such policies.

- European and international perspectives are often not included in national career information.

Questions That Policies Need To Address

- How can labour market information on occupations be harnessed for career information and guidance purposes?

- How should people's preferences for learning in different ways be taken into account in developing career information delivery systems? What should the balance be between experiential and non-experiential learning modes for career information, and for which target groups? How should different ways of providing career information (for example occupational guides, leaflets, brochures, handbooks, catalogues, promotional material, videos, films, CD-ROMs and DVDs, the Internet, the mass media) be tailored to different user needs?

- How can career information be better designed so that it is a learning tool, rather than simply a way to provide basic information?

- How should users be involved in the design and evaluation of career information delivery systems and products?

- How should career information be integrated in the teaching and learning of competencies for lifelong career development?

- What major gaps are there, if any, and for which target groups, in the provision of information to assist the making of career decisions?

- What standards should apply to the content and presentation of career information material?

- What role does the private sector play in supplying career information to the public? Can public-private partnerships, as well as outsourcing, help to address some of the challenges in the production of career information?

- What is the role of the social partners in career information development and supply?

- How should different government ministries and agencies co-operate in the development and supply of educational and occupational information?

- How is responsibility shared for the adequate collection, production and dissemination of career information, along a set of nationally agreed standards?

- Who ensures compatibility in the collection, production, linkage and dissemination of career information across different administrative regions in decentralised systems, in order to avoid fragmentation and lack of transparency?

- Do providers of career information work collaboratively to avoid overlap, and to ensure that systems are comprehensive and transparent, and connect educational, occupational and labour market supply and demand data?

- How is a European and international dimension integrated in national, regional and local career information?

- Do the available career information tools work from the questions which users want to be answered, or from the information which producers want them to have?

- Is career information evaluated regularly to assess its accessibility and impact?

Some Policy Options

- Undertake national, regional and local mapping exercises of career guidance information provided through a range of media (such as newspapers, TV) to a range of target groups (youth, employed, unemployed) in order to develop a coherent strategy for the delivery of career information to citizens.

- Develop or adapt national standards for career information.

- Establish mechanisms for co-ordinating career information across different government agencies and between the public and private sectors.

- Help industries that are experiencing skill shortages to produce useful and impartial career information.

- Examine whether the career information that is produced is used, who uses it, and if they find it useful.

- Make sure that career guidance practitioners are trained in how to use and evaluate career information.

- Invest in the training and development of career information specialists.

- Link web-based, Europe-wide and international career information systems with national information systems.

Examples of Effective Responses

▪ *Systematic labour market information:* In the Netherlands, a database of projected labour market demand in some 2,500 occupations has been developed, linked to related education and training routes.

▪ *Multi-dimensional career information systems:* Poland has developed a multi-dimensional career information system - 'Counsellor 2000' - integrating the most recent developments in artificial intelligence. It stimulates the client's efforts by linking information management with decision-making strategies. Information about educational and training pathways, and the relevant occupations they lead to, is linked to the personal profile of the client using the system, itself developed after accessing self-assessment tools available on the same software. In addition, the system has been adapted so that it can be targeted at particular groups of users, such as persons with disabilities.

▪ *Integrating career information systems:* The French IDEO (*Information documentation edition ONISEP*) project has as a goal the development of a system of information engineering for publication purposes. The project sets out to systematically and regularly renew databases used in guidance, and to link them to automatic publishing methods. ONISEP (*Office national d'information sur les enseignements et les professions*) is working on a new fast computer-based network with a view to maximising exchanges of information on the Internet, while ensuring that data transfer is fully secure. ONISEP works together with CEREQ (*Centre d'etudes et de recherche sur les qualifications*), a public organisation supervised by the public education and employment services, whose task is to develop expertise in such areas as statistics, certification, integration, occupational outlets, training-employment links, and so on.

▪ *A private-sector career information initiative:* Careers World is a widely used career information product that was developed in Ireland by the private sector with financial support from the Department of Education and Science. Available on the internet at http://www.careersworld.com/ and distributed free to schools and other educational institutions in CD-ROM format, Careers World draws its information from enterprises, most of which are large and in the private sector, and enables them to provide information on the employment and careers that they offer. It is funded by employer subscriptions, and is seen as a way for firms to help recruit staff in a tight labour market. Its coverage of small firms (which form the majority of the Irish enterprises) is limited, as is its coverage of some occupational areas. It provides links to tertiary and further education course information related to particular occupational areas. It also includes a preference assessment exercise, plus a 'real life' component: exemplars of individuals who are working in the contributing enterprises.

▪ *Quality standards:* Guidelines for career information have been developed in a number of countries, including Denmark and the Netherlands. All operate on a voluntary basis.

▪ *The European dimension in career information systems:* PLOTEUS (http://www.ploteus.org/ploteus/portal/home) is the European Union's internet portal of learning opportunities. EUROGUIDANCE (http://www.euroguidance.org.uk) is a network of guidance centres in the EU and EEA countries, and is a source of information, responding to the need of guidance workers to be familiar with other countries' education, training and guidance systems and programmes. EURES (http://europa.eu.int/eures/index.jsp) links all public employment services in the European Union and European Economic Area states, and is being developed with European Union funding to facilitate worker mobility by ensuring that information about skills shortages and surpluses for each country and region is more transparent and more accessible. ERA CAREERS (http://www.europa.eu.int/eracareers) is a portal targeted at researchers in all stages of their careers, and that provides information about research jobs, fellowships and grants throughout Europe.

TRAINING AND QUALIFICATIONS

Policy Issues

- Governments have been very inactive in defining the content and process of initial training for career guidance practitioners, and in relating these to the goals for public education, training and employment policies. As a result trainers and practitioner associations have developed training programmes quite divorced from public policy objectives.

- National reviews of training for career guidance practitioners take place very infrequently or not at all.

- Significant differences occur in the quality and types of career guidance services that users experience both within and between countries due to significant variations in the training of career guidance practitioners.

- Too often, qualifications in related fields (for example, psychology or pedagogy) are regarded as sufficient for career guidance practitioners, even though such qualifications pay little or no attention to career guidance competencies.

- There are not enough well trained career guidance practitioners to meet demand.

- There is little national data to enable proper human resource planning for career guidance practitioners and investment in training to take place.

- There is huge variation in the length of initial training programmes: ranging from three weeks to five years. Much of the very brief training that is provided is inadequate to develop the knowledge and skills needed for the job. On the other hand much of the long training that is available develops skills to provide in-depth careers intervention and psychological counselling required by only a minority of users.

- In most countries there are no graded and integrated learning pathways that enable guidance workers to progress from non-expert to expert status. Support staff in career guidance services such as information officers and community liaison staff are provided with no training.

- Too much of the current training is sector-specific, and existing qualification structures do not permit job mobility for career guidance practitioners between employment and education sectors, or even between different sectors of education in some cases.

- There are many gaps in the content of training programmes. These include: skills in ICT use; training for support staff; skills for delivering career education through the curriculum; knowledge of labour market changes; the international dimension of guidance; and how to organise and manage services.

Questions That Policies Need To Address

- Given the public policy goals that career guidance serves, and given that such services are mainly government funded, what influence does public policy have on the training of guidance practitioners? What is the role of government in deciding and monitoring the content and process of training?

- What is the role of other actors such as the social partners in the initial and continuing training of career guidance practitioners?

- What should the role of associations of career guidance practitioners and of organisations that provide the training be in decisions on the content and process of initial training? Should they only provide advice? Should they accredit programmes?

- In deciding on the content, level and duration of training, what should the balance be between: government, which sets public policy objectives for career guidance and funds it; associations that represent the interests of practitioners; and organisations that provide the training?

- Where initial training programmes for career guidance practitioners are developed autonomously by higher education institutions, how can a standard approach be developed nationally to minimise the differences in outcomes for users of career guidance services that arise from differences in the training of guidance practitioners?

- What training is required for those that work with career guidance practitioners to provide services? For example education and training providers, private consultants, teachers, school principals? How can such training complement the training of career guidance practitioners?

- How and by whom is the changing nature of the work of the career guidance practitioner being monitored so that appropriate changes or adjustments can be made to the content and process of training?

- Does the current content and process of initial and continuing training of career guidance practitioners match the demands of job? Is there, for example, an appropriate balance between psychology, pedagogy and labour market studies?

- Is the duration of training sufficient to develop the knowledge and skills that are required? What should the content of initial training be in relation to the content of continuing training?

- Do people that are hired to provide career guidance already have the knowledge and skills required to do the job? Or do they need to undertake additional training?

- Is the way that training is provided (for example: pre-service university course; in-service course; on-the-job training) effective? Is it economical?

- In the training that is available, is there an appropriate balance between knowledge and theory on the one hand and practical skills and competencies on the other?

- Are the qualifications awarded to practitioners: at too high a level; at too low a level; affordable to whomever is responsible for funding the training?

- How should the costs of initial and continuing training be shared between practitioners and those who employ them?

- Is there scope for more differentiated staffing, with wider use of trained support staff, and with career guidance practitioners acting as managers and co-ordinators of services, not just as personal service providers?

- What training might be provided to help the career progression of career guidance practitioners? Do training opportunities designed to support such progression pay adequate attention to policy issues, to the management of career guidance services, and to research?

Some Policy Options

- Build clear objectives and outcomes for career guidance programmes within overall education, training and employment policies, and use these to guide the development and monitoring of training programmes for career guidance practitioners.

- Create national training and qualifications pathways to enable career guidance practitioners to progress from non-expert to expert roles.

- Develop high quality training programmes that combine classroom-based learning with practical skills development and on-the-job experience.

- Develop targeted training for those who work with career guidance practitioners such as teachers, youth workers, community volunteers and social workers.

- Use distance learning and ICT to make training more accessible.

- Ensure that recruitment policies for publicly funded career guidance services pay attention to the knowledge and skills required for the job.

- Undertake a study of projections of supply and demand for career guidance personnel for the next 15 years.

- Work with tertiary education institutions and career guidance practitioners to develop a competency framework for all of those who provide career guidance. Make sure that this framework includes the competencies needed to deliver government policy goals, and that it covers all relevant settings in which career guidance is provided and all categories of staff. Use this framework to develop modular and cross-sectoral training programmes.

Examples of Effective Responses

- *A competence framework:* In Canada, the Standards and Guidelines for Career Development Practitioners provides a framework within which a variety of roles can be identified. It has been developed through a careful process of consultation and consensus-building. The framework outlines a number of core competencies with all career development practitioners need to have, regardless of their employment setting. It also includes a range of specialised competencies, the need for which will vary according to the nature of the service being provided, the type of work setting, and the client groups that are being served. The framework is being field-tested in a wide variety of settings to assess how it might be used (for further details, see www.career-dev-guidelines.org). The Canadian framework has strongly influenced the international standards developed by the International Association for Educational and Vocational Guidance, which provide a useful reference point for such processes in other countries.

- *A training programme:* The University of East London offers a Postgraduate Diploma in Career Guidance that can be entered by those with a recognised university degree or equivalent. It can be completed either in one year full-time or in two to three years part-time. It trains people to work with a range of client groups. Successful completion can satisfy requirements for membership of the Institute of Career Guidance (ICG). The course covers guidance theory and practice, equal opportunities (including strategies to promote equal opportunities in a career guidance context), organisation change and development (including examination of a guidance agency in the framework of organisation theory and change management), labour market studies, and education systems and practice.

- *A register of career guidance practitioners:* In Germany, the German Association for Career Counselling (DVB) has established a Register of Career Counsellors which currently has 420 members (around 100 of whom are not DVB members). To be registered, applicants have to demonstrate relevant initial qualifications, certified experience, and regular continuing training.

12

FUNDING CAREER GUIDANCE SERVICES

Policy Issues

- Career guidance services can be funded in a number of ways. These including: direct funding by central government; devolved funding to regional or local organisations; subcontracting of services; and market-based provision. The challenge is to find the most appropriate model, or mix of models, that will work in a particular context.

- Devolved funding systems raise questions about the residual responsibilities of central government. In particular, where funding is devolved by governments, questions need to be asked about how the quality and consistency of services can be ensured.

- The private market for career guidance is under-developed in most countries. Those who can afford to pay for services cannot access them privately. On the other hand many individuals who most need career guidance are least able to afford it, and least willing to pay for it. If a wider private market existed the overall level of career guidance services available to citizens would be increased. This would allow more government funds to be directed to those most in need. Hence governments need to seek ways to stimulate the development of market-based provision.

- There are big gaps in the availability of information on government expenditure on career guidance services, and on their outcomes. This makes it difficult for policy-makers to know what benefits they are getting for their investment.

Questions That Policies Need To Address

- How much does government spend on career guidance services, how does it spend it, and what does it spend it on? How can expenditure data be improved?

- How can existing investment be used more efficiently?

- What additional investment is needed for which aspects of delivery?

- Which aspects of delivery are the primary responsibility of government? Which aspects are more appropriate for private sector or joint venture investment?

- Where services are privately provided, what responsibility does government have towards them?

- What alternatives exist to government funding of career guidance services? How can such alternative sources of funds be stimulated?

- What are the limitations of stimulating private provision of career guidance, particularly in relation to equitable access to quality services? How can these limitations be addressed?

- How can the benefits of government investment in career guidance services be established in relation to their cost?

- What steps can be taken to ensure that public funding aimed at meeting the career guidance needs of at-risk groups is benefiting these targeted groups?

- When public funding is channelled towards institutions to cover a package of services, including career guidance, what measures can be taken to ensure that these institutions allocate this funding to career guidance provision? Is earmarked funding preferable to block funding in facilitating the attainment of policy targets?

- Should the state exercise a role as a guarantor of quality in the provision of a public good such as career guidance? If so, how?

Some Policy Options

- Undertake market research into citizens' demand for career guidance services and their willingness to pay for such services.

- Develop a quasi-market in the provision of career guidance services, stimulating private provision through subcontracting to the for-profit and voluntary sectors functions that have been traditionally been fulfilled by the public sector.

- Ensure that all career guidance services in receipt of public funding meet pre-established quality standards.

- Make the supply and demand for services more transparent, so that private providers may be more inclined to invest resources in this area.

- Link career guidance to mechanisms such as individual learning accounts and training levies for financing learning. Accept career guidance costs as allowable costs, alongside direct education and training costs, in such schemes.

- Explore possibilities for supporting the development and expansion of career guidance through social insurance contributions from individuals and employers, rather than directly through government budgets from tax contributions.

- Encourage employers to invest in guidance provision to address the career development needs of their employees, on the grounds that this contributes to the employers' competitiveness through the continued development of workers' skills, motivation and productivity.

- Consider, where appropriate, cost-effective alternatives to supplement face-to-face personal career guidance, including curriculum provision, group guidance, self-help services, and ICT-based services.

- Where services are devolved, guard against the problems this can produce: costly overlap; lack of co-ordination within and across sectors; a deficit in comparable standards between regions leading to inequitable access to services; and an overall degeneration in standards. Strive to find a judicious mix of centralised and decentralised models, with local units developing their own policy in the context of agreed objectives and guidelines that have been arrived at after wide consultation with stakeholders.

- Where funding to regions or to institutions takes the form of block grants, adopt strategies that require regions or institutions to earmark funds for career guidance (for example, through the use of staffing formulas).

- Where career guidance is to be encouraged through the market, plan strategies to compensate for market failure.

- Ensure that quality standards are set for the market in order to raise consumer confidence.

- Ensure that strategies are in place for collecting expenditure and resource-use data to support the development of policy.

Examples of Effective Responses

- *Devolved funding:* In Estonia, the Ministry of Education and Research signs an annual co-operation contract with each of the country's 15 administrative regions. The county governor of a specific region, in turn, can outsource career guidance services to a provider, who can be either a non-profit association or a municipal institution. The regions can decide how to use about 95% of the money addressed to youth career counselling by the Ministry of Education. The rest of the funds are earmarked for re-training, for information materials and for the maintenance of the electronic information system. The budget for in-service development of guidance staff is provided by the local government. While there are no mandatory service standards, there are specific guidelines which providers are asked to follow. In the case of the Ministry of Social Affairs, salaries for workers and for the equipment used in providing career guidance come from the state budget. Supplementary funds, stemming from the proceeds of privatisation, are earmarked for the re-training of career counsellors and of job mediation consultants, for the publication of career information brochures, and for the purchase of career tests and training in their use. Funding from the European Union programme PHARE 2000 supports a project on 'Support to the balanced development of labour market services', which involves staff training, and the development of the career guidance system and of service standards in career guidance. The latter are applicable across the board.

13

CO-ORDINATION AND STRATEGIC LEADERSHIP

Policy Issues

- In most countries education, training and employment policies take little account of the importance of career guidance.

- Most countries need to provide stronger strategic leadership so that career guidance services can be better planned and better co-ordinated:

  - ➢ Services within the education, training, employment, community and private sectors are fragmented: rarely well co-ordinated, coherently planned, or well integrated.

  - ➢ Too often the requirements of institutions or the needs of practitioners, rather than user needs, determine what services are provided and how they are provided.

  - ➢ In developing and planning career guidance services there is a lack of effective collaboration both between different government departments, and between government and other stakeholders.

  - ➢ Social partners and stakeholders other than government have no role in the development of guidance policies and in service provision.

- As a result, people who need career guidance can find it difficult to get access to services that meet their needs, and services are inconsistent between sectors such as education and employment.

- Few countries have developed policy structures to ensure that the different sub-systems that provide career guidance are connected to each other, through such means as inter-ministerial or inter-departmental committees, national guidance forums, or a policy unit which has the whole system of provision as its remit. Adopting a lifelong perspective on learning and employability in order to plan services would provide a framework to help overcome fragmentation.

- Better strategic leadership is even more crucial, if harder to achieve, in decentralised systems. In decentralised systems it is needed in order to guarantee equitable access to services, and comparable standards in service delivery.

- Legislation that relates to career guidance rarely addresses citizens' entitlements to services or the standards that services should meet. Often legislation refers only to the provision of services in very general terms, and is limited to single sectors such as education or the labour market.

Questions That Policies Need To Address

- How well do policies for education, training and employment reflect the need for and importance of career guidance?

- How can a lifelong learning policy framework be used to bring coherence to guidance provision across education, training and employment sectors?

- What strategies need to be developed in order to make the existing subsystems in which guidance provision is placed more coherent internally and to make such provision more identifiable and accessible to users?

- How can cross-sectoral collaboration between the different government departments responsible for career guidance be promoted and enhanced?

- What are the financial, resource and organisational implications of transforming a fragmented age- and sector-specific approach to career guidance provision to one that is integrated in a lifelong learning framework and that allows a diverse range of services to be provided throughout the lifespan within such a framework?

- Given government priorities and policy objectives, what goals should be articulated for career guidance services?

- Which policy levers are available to steer career guidance provision across the life span? How can they be improved?

- What changes are required to existing legislation or other steering instruments in order to adapt them to a lifelong learning policy framework?

- If existing legislation does not cover career guidance provision, what other policy documents can steer such provision?

- How should citizen service entitlement be reflected in legislation or other steering documents for career guidance provision?

- How can present legislation, if provision-driven and obliging providers to offer a service, be adapted to empower citizens by specifying their entitlements to a service?

- What are the main gaps in career guidance provision, and how can these gaps be addressed through co-operation between ministries, sectors and subsystems?

- What mechanisms exist to ensure quality and consistency in service delivery within and across sectors? Are these provisions mandatory, and if so, which inspection and monitoring strategies have been developed? How can cross-sectoral collaboration in quality assurance be developed and enhanced?

- How can users, providers and other stakeholders be involved in the development of policies in career guidance?

Some Policy Options

- Benchmark existing national, regional and local provision of career guidance against lifelong learning policy objectives.

- Build the notion of an integrated, lifelong and comprehensive career guidance service into the lifelong learning policies that are being developed.

- Explore possibilities for greater collaboration and cooperation between career guidance services within and across sectors at all levels.

- Revise the relevant legislative frameworks for education, training and employment, ensuring that they specifically address career guidance, particularly from the perspective of the citizen, in a lifelong learning context.

- Establish an inter-departmental structure that brings together different government portfolios with a responsibility for career guidance provision. Use this to develop common government policy objectives for guidance and greater coherence, more efficiency, and sharing of responsibilities in guidance provision.

- Set up a national forum for guidance policy and systems development which includes both government and stakeholder representatives, as well as key partners in service provision, in order to help focus and develop agendas and to steer policy making.

- In countries with strong, decentralised regions, establish regional guidance forums as a subset of national forum activities.

- Develop policies, systems and practices for career guidance provision through mutual learning and international collaboration using the possibilities offered by European Union education, training and employment programmes, the European Social Fund, and World Bank investment.

Examples of Effective Responses

- *Legislation concerning career guidance services:* Some legislation specifically indicates the types of service that are to be provided, and to whom. In Germany the Framework Act for Higher Education requires institutions of higher education to 'inform students and applicants on the opportunities and conditions of study and on the content, structure and requirements of study courses' and during the entire study period to 'assist students by providing subject-oriented advice'. In providing such guidance, it also requires institutions to co-operate with 'the authorities responsible for vocational guidance'.

- *Improving cross-sectoral collaboration and involvement of social partners in the development of career guidance policies:* In Finland, key stakeholders engage in wide-ranging and many-sided co-operative ventures, and several organisations are interested in issues connected with career guidance. A national advisory group has been active since the 1980s, with a mandate from the ministries of education and of labour and with a broad membership including the social partners. It has reported biennially on guidance in secondary and vocational education, and on issues relating to the transitions from comprehensive to secondary education and from education to the labour market. It has also presented proposals for disseminating good practice and for filling gaps in provision. There have been discussions about extending its mandate to cover lifelong guidance.

- *Developing an integrated system of lifelong career guidance:* In 2001 the National Assembly for Wales launched Careers Wales, an all-age career guidance service that operates through a confederation of seven regional careers companies with a common brand name. The service's vision statement sees career guidance as being at the heart of social and economic prosperity, and its mission statement reflects a belief in the development of people through lifelong career planning. Careers Wales is responsible for delivering the statutory careers service for youth, adult guidance, the *learndirect* call centre network, the Youth Gateway (a short, intensive transition skills course for at-risk 16-17 year-olds), and education-business links. It also supports school and college career education programmes (mandatory in Wales for those aged 13-19) through curriculum consultancy, teacher training, and support for careers libraries. Its one-stop shops are accessible on a drop-in basis to all ages. Further outreach services to adults are delivered in a wide variety of community settings, some using a mobile facility, some by telephone, and some online. Staff employed by Careers Wales can work with both youth and adults, though they tend to specialise in one or the other. Having a common employing authority for all staff gives managers flexibility to deploy staff across different areas of specialisation and to extend their experience.

14

ENSURING THE QUALITY OF CAREER GUIDANCE

Policy Issues

- There is little regular and systematic evaluation of the quality of career guidance services in most countries. Standards for the quality of services do not exist or are present in some sectors but not in others. Where quality standards exist, they tend to be voluntary rather than mandatory. Inspection of services against these quality standards is the exception rather than the rule. Only occasionally do quality standards have checking procedures or sanctions attached to them.

- There are no standards or controls in private sector provision of career guidance services. Where guidance services are subcontracted by the public sector to the private or voluntary sectors, standards of service and outcomes for users are generally not specified. Where governments have decentralised or devolved career guidance services, quality frameworks to ensure that central policy goals and standards are attained have rarely been established.

- In the absence of quality frameworks, there is an over-reliance on staff qualifications or professional codes of practice to assure quality. Frequently these cover some forms of provision but not others. In centralised systems where administrative controls are used to ensure quality, problems often arise because of the variable or inadequate qualifications of staff.

- Much of the quantitative information that is available about career guidance provision has limited usefulness for evaluating processes and service quality.

- Career guidance policies are insufficiently guided by user feedback and by relevant evidence and data, including such basic information as levels of usage and types of services accessed.

Questions That Policies Need To Address

- Why is the evaluation of publicly funded career guidance services important for users and for taxpayers? How are the interests of users and taxpayers served through such evaluation?

- Given the current status of guidance provision in your country, what should appropriate evaluation mechanisms be? Who should have a say in this and how?

- What are the advantages and limitations of (i) administrative-centred, (ii) user-centred, and (iii) practitioner-centred quality assurance mechanisms? Which combination of these produces the best outcomes?

- What are the advantages and limitations of voluntary versus mandatory quality assurance standards?

- How appropriate and adequate are general quality standard frameworks such as ISO or Total Quality Management for career guidance services? How do we know?

- What good examples of quality assurance for career guidance have been developed at national or sectoral level that can be modified and transferred to other contexts?

- How is career guidance in the private sector evaluated and regulated? What should the role of government be?

- What kinds of data are presently available that would help in gaining insight into the quality of services?

- What use is made of regular evaluation processes like user feedback?

- Which stakeholders and representative organisations need to be involved in designing and monitoring service standards? How can users be involved in this process? How are stakeholders' interests (users, taxpayers, administrators, practitioners) represented in existing quality assurance frameworks? How should such interests be better represented?

- What mechanisms have been developed to ensure consistency of service delivery across different sectors, different regions, and different providers?

- What quality standards need to be developed in order to ensure that career information is produced in a reliable, objective, timely, comprehensive and user-friendly manner?

Some Policy Options

- Investigate the evaluation mechanisms and quality assurance frameworks for career guidance, including quality frameworks for career information materials, that are being used in your country. How can they be improved?

- Investigate the evaluation mechanisms and quality assurance frameworks for career guidance, including quality frameworks for career information materials, which are being used in other countries. What lessons can be learned from their experiences?

- Investigate quality assurance frameworks and methods that are used in other areas of education, training and employment, and in consumer rights policies in your country. Evaluate how relevant or appropriate these are for adaptation or use with career guidance services.

- Pilot test a range of evaluation procedures for career guidance services. Identify which gives the best outcomes for the user, the taxpayer, and the funder.

- Initiate cross-sectoral discussions on evaluation processes and quality assurance frameworks with relevant stakeholders (users, taxpayers, administrators and practitioners) and together develop a strategy to improve existing evaluation procedures. Identify how different sectors can support each other in developing such a strategy and how they can learn from each others' experiences. Develop common approaches as appropriate.

- Consider how standards could be used to accredit career guidance services. Consider how such an approach could be supported by the branding of accredited services, using this as a technique for marketing them more effectively.

- Establish quality standards against statements of service for clients (including access to services by priority client groups), and introduce user monitoring and feedback mechanisms to ensure that such standards are met.

- Use quality standards as criteria for establishing performance targets (including targets for access to services by priority client groups), for organising service evaluation and inspection, and as monitoring and feedback mechanisms.

- When the delivery of career guidance is devolved (either through outsourcing or through decentralisation), establish minimum standards which must be met by those regional and local authorities or other third parties such as community groups that are publicly funded to provide services.

- Improve the quality of services by requiring higher standards in the initial and in-service training of the different categories of career guidance staff.

- Undertake or commission studies of the work carried out by career guidance staff and those involved in the production of career information, in both the education and labour market sectors, to identify the competencies that practitioners are expected to demonstrate.

- Develop measures of the skills and competencies that career guidance services are seeking to develop in clients, and examine ways of building such measures into quality standards.

- Involve users in the design, implementation and evaluation of quality-assurance systems.

- Where career guidance is part of an overall evaluation of institutions and agencies (such as schools, vocational education settings, universities or employment offices), ensure that the inspection team includes persons who understand, and have competence in, career guidance. Develop specific criteria to be used for the inspection of career guidance within such settings, and either publish separate reports, or have a substantial sub-section dedicated to career guidance in the overall report.

- Consider how quality assurance frameworks developed for publicly funded career guidance can be applied to private sector provision to ensure user protection.

Examples of Effective Responses

- *Quality standards:* In the United Kingdom, quality standards for career guidance delivery were initially developed by the Guidance Council, an independent organisation representing career guidance organisations, and are now managed by the Employment National Training Organisation. The *matrix* Quality Standard, as it is now known, covers five areas that directly concern the ways that individuals are helped (for example, how effectively they are helped to explore options and make choices, or to gain access to information) and five areas that concern the ways that services are managed (for example, how well they make use of client feedback, or develops their staff's skills). Career guidance organisations wishing to be accredited against the Standard are assessed by an external body, currently the Guidance Accreditation Board. Organisations wishing to receive government funds for career guidance provision must possess such accreditation. The Standard can also be used for quality improvement, with the aid of consultants from the Guidance Council. For further details of the *matrix* Standard, see: www.matrix-quality-standard.com

- *Voluntary guidelines:* In Denmark, following the publication of ethical guidelines in 1995 by the then National Council for Educational and Vocational Guidance, additional guidelines have been published for the development of quality-assurance processes. These suggest that each service should discuss and agree upon quality criteria and set up appropriate self-assessment procedures.

15

ASSESSING THE EFFECTIVENESS OF CAREER GUIDANCE

Policy Issues

- At present, few governments have the data needed to provide an overall picture of career guidance provision, or of its effectiveness in meeting public policy objectives.

- Few government ministries are able to state precisely how much public money is being spent on career guidance services or how it is spent. Information about private investment and expenditure in this field is not available.

- Most policy makers rely on a very limited evidence base when evaluating the inputs, processes and outputs of career guidance services.

- Where data is collected, the tendency is to focus on simple quantitative indicators (such as the number of users interviewed by guidance services, success rates in job placements by public employment services) rather than more policy-relevant indicators such as client satisfaction or improved career decision making skills.

- The task of establishing a reliable evidence base is particularly challenging in the career guidance field, where the process and outcomes are neither readily visible nor easily measured, and where causality is difficult to determine.

- Despite a strong research tradition in the career guidance field, there are few researchers and specialised research centres specifically addressing methodological and other issues related to the generation of a sound evidence base with direct policy relevance. The little research that exists remains fragmented and is not cumulative in nature.

- Even where an evidence base is being built up, the link between such data and the policy making process is often tenuous.

Questions That Policies Need To Address

- What benefits will result from having a better evidence base for making career guidance policies? Who will benefit? How?

- What data is currently being collected, by whom, across which sectors, and for which purposes? How is this data used to guide policy making and evaluation (if at all)? Which are the data gaps that need to be filled?

- Where administrative information systems are in place, what changes are needed to include guidance-related data? Are systems operated by the education and labour market authorities compatible, and can the data on the different systems be consolidated?

- In decentralised systems, what strategies exist to ensure that information gathered at a regional or sub-system level can be consolidated at a national level (for example to monitor consistency of services and equal access to entitlements)?

- What new kinds of data are required to monitor the match between the career guidance that is provided and policy objectives?

- What data-gathering strategies are in place to signal needs for new, different or expanded services and target groups?

- What evidence exists of the return from current public investment in career guidance services?

- What are the relative costs and benefits of different types of services?

- What information is available on the extent and nature of private sector provision of career guidance? Who uses such services and at what cost?

- Are data being collected for both publicly and privately funded guidance services on:

  - The numbers of users of guidance services and their characteristics (such as age, gender, region, socioeconomic status, educational level and ethnic origin);

  - The different needs of different types of users;

  - User satisfaction rates; and

  - Variation in these rates by user characteristics?

Some Policy Options

- Identify the range of evidence currently being collected for different dimensions of career guidance provision, and the purpose, use and usefulness of such data.

- Identify gaps in the evidence needed to measure the impact of current investment in career guidance. Consider which other types of data are now required.

- Collaborate with stakeholders (users, administrators, practitioners) at national level to identify which types of data, and what procedures for data collection, would be needed to improve data on the impact of career guidance upon the achievement of public policy goals. (Examples might include indicators on users, services provided, staff time-use, and costs and outcomes.)

- Investigate what range, types and procedures for data collection are currently being used in other countries and adapt or adopt these as appropriate.

- Collaborate with other countries in developing common indicators, benchmarks and approaches to data collection and methods for cost-benefit studies.

- Provide research funding to identify the kinds of evidence that are required for the development of sound policies in career guidance. Commission research and evaluation studies.

- Ensure that research being commissioned for education, training and employment policy implementation and evaluation includes a strong reference to career guidance provision.

- Ensure that statistical staff in ministries are aware of the measurement and evaluation issues involved in career guidance provision. Initiate discussions between such staff and those responsible for career guidance policy.

- Encourage, where feasible, the setting up of a research unit that focuses specifically on career guidance issues in order to strengthen the evidence base required to inform policy development.

- Fund academic researchers, including those who work in the field of career guidance, to undertake research to support evidence-based policy making for career guidance.

- Ensure that initial career guidance training programmes include a strong component on evidence-based policymaking. Provide in-service training in this area to career guidance practitioners.

- Build questions about career guidance services into surveys being carried out nationally and or regionally on topics such as household use of services and products, the labour force, adult education, or school-leavers. Explore possibilities for market surveys to throw light on people's career guidance needs, and on where and how these needs are currently being met.

Examples of Effective Responses

- *Linking evaluation and policy development:* During 2000-03 Finland conducted a wide-ranging evaluation of its guidance services: in comprehensive schools; in secondary education; in tertiary education; in adult education; and in the public employment service. While revealing many examples of good practice, the evaluations indicated that national policies were fragmented, and that services had not been able to meet growing demand. Feedback mechanisms were found to be weak at the institutional level, and a need was revealed for stronger planning and leadership in guidance delivery. The outcomes of the review process have been translated into policy in a number of ways. For example, the variability in tertiary services revealed by the review has resulted in the relationship between funding and career guidance being tightened, with institutions being required to prepare guidance plans as part of their performance contracts. The National Board of Education is to execute new national guidelines for guidance in schools, and to implement a web-based service to support the institutional self-evaluation of services. Other initiatives include strengthening in-service training for teachers and guidance practitioners, creating a network of regional consultants, introducing a number of regional pilot programmes, and developing national standards for student-counsellor ratios.

- *Specialised career guidance centres that undertake research:*

➢ In the Czech Republic, the National Institute of Vocational Education has conducted extensive research on student use of and satisfaction with a range of career guidance services. These include both services provided by schools and services provided for schools by external agencies, by sources such as the media and the Internet, and by informal sources such as families and friends.

➢ Ireland has a National Centre for Guidance in Education, an agency of the Department of Education and Science. Its roles include managing national initiatives, developing guidance support materials for practitioners, providing advice on good practice, supporting innovation and pilot projects, disseminating information to practitioners, organising in-service training, commissioning and carrying out surveys and research on guidance, and advising the Department on policy development.

➢ Romania has an Educational and Vocational Department at the Institute for Educational Sciences, which has been designated as the methodological authority for the Ministry of Education's guidance and counselling network. It is run by a team of highly qualified scholars with advanced degrees in a variety of areas linked to guidance and counselling. It has conducted a number of evaluative research projects on human and ICT resources, staff qualifications, tests, career guidance for adults, computerised career guidance programmes, and beneficiaries of guidance services.

➢ In the United Kingdom, specialised centres for research and policy analysis in career guidance include the National Institute for Careers Education and Counselling (NICEC) and the Centre for Guidance Studies at the University of Derby. Several other centres, both within tertiary education and outside it, employ research staff with a specific expertise in career guidance. The department for Education and Skills in England has sponsored the establishment of a National Research Forum for career guidance. The Forum brings together the key players in career guidance research to improve the capacity, coherence, quality and co-ordination of research on career guidance in the United Kingdom. It will act as a focus for dialogue between researchers, service providers, practitioner organisations and policy makers to promote a much stronger evidence base for policy formulation and for practice.

16

CONCLUSION: THE FEATURES OF A LIFELONG GUIDANCE SYSTEM

A commitment to lifelong learning and active employment policies requires OECD and European Union member countries to meet two key challenges in building lifelong guidance systems. These are to:

➤ Move from an approach that emphasises assistance with immediate occupational and educational decisions to a broader approach that also develops people's ability to manage their own careers: developing career planning and employability skills; and

➤ Find cost effective ways to expand citizens' access to career guidance throughout the lifespan.

Lifelong guidance systems that meet these challenges need to have a number of features. These are:

➤ Transparency and ease of access over the lifespan, including a capacity to meet the needs of a diverse range of citizens;

➤ Particular attention to key transition points over the lifespan;

➤ Flexibility and innovation in service delivery to reflect the different needs and circumstances of diverse client groups;

➤ Programmes to develop people's career-management skills;

➤ Opportunities to investigate and experience learning and work opportunities before choosing; them;

➤ Access to comprehensive and integrated educational, occupational and labour market information;

➤ Access to individual guidance by appropriately trained and qualified practitioners for those who need such help, at times when they need it;

➤ Assured access to services that are independent of the interests of particular institutions or enterprises;

➤ Processes to stimulate regular review and planning; and

➤ Involvement of relevant stakeholders.

Annex 2 sets out in more detail some of the principles that should underpin these features.

This handbook has set out a number of the specific policy issues that need to be dealt with in building systems that have these features. It has outlined some of the questions that policy makers need to ask themselves in dealing with these issues, and some of the options that are open to them. It has provided some practical examples of response that individual countries have made to these issues and questions.

ANNEX 1

ON-LINE RESOURCES FOR CAREER GUIDANCE POLICY MAKERS

1. CEDEFOP Resources

CEDEFOP (the European Centre for the Development of Vocational Training) has a range of on-line resources to assist career guidance policy makers.

1.1 Information on European Union policies, studies and projects relating to guidance

CEDEFOP's web site on guidance contains: the results of the work of the Commission's Lifelong Guidance Expert Group; information on related European Union policy developments and programmes; the results of country career guidance policy reviews carried out by the OECD, CEDEFOP and the ETF; and papers from past international guidance events and information about forthcoming events. The web site contains a link to CEDEFOP's Knowledge Management System *eKnowVet* database that enables users to search for and extract data from national career guidance policy reviews by theme across all or a selected group of the 29 European countries that took part in the reviews. There are also links to web sites with additional information on the reviews. A section with examples of interesting policy and practice will be developed on the site.

To access the guidance web-pages please go to http://www.trainingvillage.gr/etv/ and take a few minutes to register. Give your name, choose a login name, choose a password, confirm the password, give your e-mail address and country, select a language and state the position you hold in your organisation. (If you wish, you can choose to be included in the CEDEFOP Electronic Training Village's "ETV's Who's Who). Once you have registered you are invited to login with your new user name and password. You then select **projects** and **networks** and **guidance** and you will see the current web-pages.

You only need to register once: after initial registration the system remembers you, enabling you to access the pages directly using the following link:

http://www.trainingvillage.gr/etv/Projects_Networks/Guidance/

For further information contact Jennifer Wannan at CEDEFOP: *jwa@cedefop.eu.int*

1.2 The CEDEFOP virtual community

CEDEFOP also provides a virtual community addressed to policy makers, practitioners and researchers who wish to take part in active exchanges of views and information on a range of guidance themes. To join the virtual community, use the following link:

http://cedefop.communityzero.com/lifelong_guidance

2. OECD Resources

The OECD review of national career guidance policies contains a range of material that is relevant to career guidance policy makers. The material includes responses to the national questionnaires produced by participating countries, country notes written by expert teams that visited these countries, a set of eight expert papers commissioned jointly by the OECD and the European Commission, and a range of other discussion papers. The material can be accessed at http://www.oecd.org/edu/careerguidance.

ANNEX 2

COMMON AIMS AND PRINCIPLES OF LIFELONG GUIDANCE PROVISION

Introduction

The text below represents a set of common aims and principles for lifelong guidance provision agreed under the auspices of the European Union's Education and Training 2010 work programme. They have been produced in cooperation with the European Commission's Expert Group on Lifelong Guidance. The development of common aims and principles for lifelong guidance provision at European level to support national policy and systems development was recommended in the Interim Report "Education and Training 2010" of the European Council (Education/Youth) and the European Commission (2004) and was noted in the Council Resolution (Education/Youth) of May 2004 on strengthening policies, systems and practices for lifelong guidance in Europe. The Resolution prioritised the centrality of the individual/learner in the provision of such services, and the needs to (i) refocus provision to develop individuals' career competency, (ii) widen access to services and (iii) improve the quality of the services. The principles for guidance provision that follow are grouped according to those priorities.

1. What Does Lifelong Guidance Mean?

Guidance refers to a range of activities[3] that enable citizens of any age, and at any point in their lives, to: identify their capacities, competencies and interests; make meaningful educational, training and occupational decisions; and to manage their individual life paths in learning, work and other settings in which these capacities and competencies are learned and or used. Guidance is provided in a range of settings: education, training, employment, community, and private.

2. Aims

Guidance aims to:

➢ Enable **citizens** to manage and plan their learning and work pathways in accordance with their life goals, relating their competencies and interests to education, training and labour market opportunities and to self-employment, thus contributing to their personal fulfilment;

➢ Assist **educational and training institutions** to have well motivated pupils, students and trainees who take responsibility for their own learning and set their own goals for achievement;

---

[3] Examples of such activities include information and advice giving, counselling, competence assessment, mentoring, advocacy, and teaching career decision-making and career management skills. A variety of terms is used in different countries to describe these activities. These terms include educational, vocational or career guidance, guidance and counselling, occupational guidance, and counselling. To avoid ambiguity, the term "guidance" is used in the text to identify any or all of these forms of provision. Countries should interpret the term as referring to the appropriate provision in their own countries.

> ➢ Assist **enterprises and organisations** to have well motivated, employable and adaptable staff, capable of accessing and benefiting from learning opportunities both within and outside the workplace;

> ➢ Provide **policymakers** with an important means to achieve a wide range of public policy goals;

> ➢ Support local, regional, national and European **economies** through workforce development and adaptation to changing economic demands and social circumstances;

> ➢ Assist in the development of **societies** in which citizens actively contribute to their social, democratic and sustainable development.

3. Principles of Guidance Provision

The following principles underlie the provision of guidance:

Centrality of the beneficiary

> ➢ **Independence** – the guidance provided respects the freedom of the career choice and personal development of the citizen /user;

> ➢ **Impartiality** – the guidance provided is in accordance with the citizen's interests only, is not influenced by provider, institutional and funding interests, and does not discriminate on the basis of gender, age, ethnicity, social class, qualifications, ability etc;

> ➢ **Confidentiality** – citizens have a right to the privacy of personal information they provide in the guidance process;

> ➢ **Equal opportunities** – the guidance provided promotes equal opportunities in learning and work for all citizens;

> ➢ **Holistic approach** – the personal, social, cultural and economic context of a citizen's decision-making is valued in the guidance provided.

Enabling citizens

> ➢ **Active involvement** – guidance is a collaborative activity between the citizen and the provider and other significant actors (e.g. learning providers, enterprises, family members, community interests) and builds on the active involvement of the citizen;

> ➢ **Empowerment** – the guidance provided assists citizens to become competent at planning and managing their learning and career paths and the transitions therein.

Improving access

> ➢ **Transparency** – the nature of the guidance service(s) provided is immediately apparent to the citizen;

> ➢ **Friendliness and empathy** – guidance staff provide a welcoming atmosphere for the citizens;

> ➢ **Continuity** – the guidance provided supports citizens through the range of learning, work, societal and personal transitions they undertake and/or encounter;

➤ **Availability** – all citizens have a right to access guidance services[4]at any point in their lives;

➤ **Accessibility** – the guidance provided is accessible in a flexible and user friendly way such as face to face, telephone, e-mail, outreach, and is available at times and in places that suit citizens' needs;

➤ **Responsiveness** – guidance is provided through a wide range of methods to meet the diverse needs of citizens.

Assuring quality

➤ **Appropriateness of guidance methods** – the guidance methods used have a theoretical and/or scientific basis, relevant to the purpose for which they are used;

➤ **Continuous improvement** – guidance services have a culture of continuous improvement involving regular citizen feedback and provide opportunities for staff for continuous training;

➤ **Right of redress** – citizens have an entitlement to complain through a formal procedure if they deem the guidance they have received to be unsatisfactory;

➤ **Competent staff** – staff providing guidance have nationally accredited competencies to identify and address the citizen's needs, and where appropriate, to refer the citizen to more suitable provision/service.

4. European Union Policy Goals that Lifelong Guidance contributes to

Lifelong guidance assists policymakers in Europe to achieve a number of common policy goals:

➤ **Efficient investment in education and training**: Increasing the rates of participation in and of completion of education and training through improved matching of individuals' interests and abilities with learning opportunities;

➤ **Labour market efficiency**: Improving work performance and motivation, rates of job retention, reducing time spent in job search and time spent unemployed through improved matching of individual's competencies and interests with work and career development opportunities, through raising awareness of current and future employment and learning opportunities, including self employment and entrepreneurship, and through geographical and occupational mobility;

➤ **Lifelong learning**: Facilitating personal development and employability of all citizens through continuous engagement with education and training, assisting them to find their way through increasingly diversified but linked learning pathways, to identify their transferable skills, and to validate their non-formal and informal learning;

---

[4] **EUROPEAN SOCIAL CHARTER (1996 Revision) Article 9 –** The right to vocational guidance

"With a view to ensuring the effective exercise of the right to vocational guidance, the Parties undertake to provide or promote, as necessary, a service which will assist all persons, including the handicapped, to solve problems related to occupational choice and progress, with due regard to the individual's characteristics and their relation to occupational opportunity: this assistance should be available free of charge, both to young persons, including schoolchildren, and to adults."

> ➤ **Social inclusion**: Assisting the educational, social and economic integration and reintegration of all citizens and groups including third country nationals, especially those who have difficulties in accessing and understanding information about learning and work, leading to social inclusion, active citizenship and to a reduction in long-term unemployment and poverty cycles;

> ➤ **Social equity**: Assisting citizens to overcome gender, ethnic, age, disability, social class and institutional barriers to learning and work;

> ➤ **Economic development**: Supporting higher work participation rates and enhancing the up-skilling of the workforce for the knowledge-based economy and society.

ANNEX 3

SOME COMMON CRITERIA USED TO ASSESS THE QUALITY OF CAREER GUIDANCE

The criteria described below are based on the findings of a study of European career guidance quality assurance systems that was undertaken by CEDEFOP in 2003-4. They combine criteria that were found to be common to a diverse range of existing quality assurance frameworks used for guidance and criteria considered to be relevant and desirable for inclusion in any such framework.

1. Citizen and User Involvement

Quality assurance systems for career guidance should:

➢ Include information for users regarding their entitlements (for example through users' charters) and take account of the work of national and European consumer associations in processes for consumer protection and redress.

➢ Ensure that individual users are regularly consulted on their satisfaction with, and experience of, the service.

➢ Require service providers to make systematic use of the findings from such consultations.

➢ Involve the user in the design, management and evaluation of guidance services and products.

2. Practitioner Competence

Quality assurance systems for career guidance should:

➢ Require practitioners to have the competence needed to perform the guidance tasks they are called on to undertake;

➢ Require guidance practitioners to hold, or be working towards, qualifications that ensure that they have the required competencies to undertake the necessary guidance tasks;

➢ Include the monitoring or assessment of the work of guidance practitioners with respect to the outcomes of guidance interventions that they are expected to deliver;

➢ Require on-going professional development and service improvement;

➢ Include all relevant practitioner associations in the development of standards and quality assurance procedures.

3. Service Improvement

Quality assurance systems for career guidance should:

> ➢ Include clearly defined standards of service[5], some way of monitoring whether a service meets those standards, and, where this is not the case, a procedure to follow to bring them up to standard;

> ➢ Include some way of monitoring and evaluating whether action undertaken to improve services and information, in fact, results in reaching specified standards and in ongoing improvement;

> ➢ Include some way of differentiating and monitoring service provision in relation to the needs of different target groups;

> ➢ Require services to form working links with, and provide support for, groups and bodies that offer guidance informally (such as parents, voluntary organisations or bodies associated with leisure activities);

> ➢ Ensure that guidance materials used (for example assessment tools) meet quality assurance technical specifications.

4. Coherence

Quality assurance systems for career guidance should:

> ➢ Include links to promote effective working relationships within and across government departments on quality assurance in guidance;

> ➢ Ensure there are no conflicts between different quality assurance systems operating in different guidance sectors, or in relation to different target groups;

> ➢ Include ways of monitoring the use and usefulness of links between guidance-providing agencies.

5. Independent Provision

Quality assurance systems for career guidance should contain guidelines on guidance activities undertaken by private agencies, employers, trade unions and other non-State providers.

---

[5]   Standards of service should apply both to direct services to users, and to information (whether printed, through ICT or in some other format) provided to users.

ANNEX 4

THE KEY FEATURES OF A LIFELONG GUIDANCE SYSTEM

This Annex describes the key features of a lifelong guidance system. Produced by the European Commission's Expert Group on Lifelong Guidance, it is intended to be used by policy makers as a checklist for self- and peer-review at national level. It represents an ideal model of a lifelong guidance system against which the features of existing national systems can be assessed. It is intended to be used in conjunction with the common aims and principles for lifelong guidance that are set out in Annex 2 and the criteria for the assessment of the quality of career guidance that are set out in Annex 3.

1. Citizen-centred Features

➢ All citizens have access to guidance throughout their lives: at times, in locations, and in forms that respond to their needs.

➢ Citizens are provided with opportunities to learn how to make meaningful educational and occupational decisions and how to manage their learning and work so that they can progress through diverse learning opportunities and career[6] pathways.

➢ Mechanisms exist to allow citizens to: invest efficiently in and benefit from lifelong learning opportunities; identify competences gained from non-formal and informal learning; and develop other competences.

➢ Citizens' participation in guidance is enhanced through the application of principles for lifelong guidance provision such as those set out in *Annex 2*.

➢ Citizens' entitlements to guidance are clearly defined.

➢ Citizens are referred for additional guidance assistance, as appropriate, within and across sectors, and across national boundaries.

➢ Continuous improvement of guidance services, of career information, and of guidance tools and products is promoted through the application of quality assurance mechanisms, such as those set out in Annex 3, in which the citizen and user plays a key role.

2. Policy Development Features

➢ Lifelong learning and the development of employability are the guiding principles and frameworks for the development of policies, systems and practices for lifelong guidance;

➢ Policies and programmes for lifelong guidance are an integral part of national and European Community level social and economic development policies and programmes. These include

---

[6] Career refers to pathways in life in which competences are learned and used. The term covers life-wide experiences both formal (education, work) and informal (home, community).

policies and programmes relating to education, training, employment, social inclusion, gender equity, human resource development, regional and rural development, and improving living and working conditions;

➢ Guidance policies and programmes are developed in a coordinated way across education, training, employment and community sectors within a lifelong learning and active employability framework;

➢ The roles and responsibilities of all those who develop lifelong guidance policies, systems and programmes are clearly defined;

➢ Policies and programmes for lifelong guidance are formulated and implemented through stakeholder participation in mechanisms such as national forums for guidance. Relevant stakeholders include ministries, users, social partners, service providers, employment services, education and training institutions, guidance practitioners, parents, and youth;

➢ Policies and programmes for lifelong guidance take into account national and international economic change and technological development. They are reviewed periodically in relation to current and planned social and economic development.

3. System Co-ordination Features

➢ Guidance systems operate in an open, flexible and complementary way across education, training, employment and community sectors;

➢ Guidance services within one sector are coordinated with services in other sectors at national, regional and local levels. Close co-operation and co-ordination exist between guidance provided outside of the education and training system and guidance provided within it;

➢ Formal networks and partnerships of guidance providers are established at the local level;

➢ Guidance in the workplace is delivered by partnerships between education and training providers, public employment services, enterprises, and organisations that represent workers;

➢ Representatives of the social partners and other stakeholders are included in the bodies responsible for governing publicly funded guidance services;

➢ In decentralised structures, central arrangements exist to ensure consistency in regional and local services so that all citizens benefit equally, regardless of geographical location.

4. Targeting Within Universal Provision

➢ Measures are taken to provide effective and adequate guidance for learning and work for groups who are at risk of social exclusion such as: persons who did not complete compulsory schooling or who left school without qualifications; women; older workers; members of linguistic and other minority groups; persons with disabilities; migrant workers; and workers in fragile economic sectors and enterprises who are at risk of unemployment. The goal of these measures is to help these groups to enjoy equality in employment and improved integration into society and the economy.

➢ Such measures are part of national, regional and local strategies for universal lifelong guidance provision.

5. Review Features

➢ Guidance systems and programmes are periodically reviewed in order to:

✓ Make the best use of available resources;

✓ Promote synergy within and across education, training and employment sectors;

✓ Adjust their organisation, content and methods in light of: changing social and economic conditions; the changing needs of particular groups; and advances in relevant knowledge; and

✓ Make any changes that are required for the effectiveness of national policies.

➢ Research is undertaken to support evidence-based policy and systems development.

➢ Research and experimental guidance programmes are designed in order to:

✓ Evaluate the internal efficiency and external effectiveness of individual components of the lifelong guidance system;

✓ Determine the direct and indirect costs and benefits of alternative patterns and methods of providing lifelong guidance;

✓ Determine criteria for setting priorities and establishing strategies for the development of lifelong guidance for particular sectors of economic activity and for particular groups of the population;

✓ Increase knowledge of the psychological, sociological and pedagogical aspects of lifelong guidance;

✓ Improve the psychological tests and other methods used for the identification of competences, the appraisal of aptitudes and interests, and the assessment of levels of knowledge and skill attained through non-formal and informal learning;

✓ Assess employment opportunities in the various sectors of economic activity and occupations; and

✓ Improve available information on occupations, their requirements and career progression pathways.

➢ Administrative arrangements and methods are designed and modified so that they support the implementation of lifelong guidance programmes.

6. International Features

➢ Europe is the reference field for the provision of lifelong guidance services within the European Union.

➢ Member states co-operate with each other, with the European Commission and with other stakeholders in planning, elaborating and implementing collaborative action in lifelong guidance within the context of Community policies and programmes for education, training and employment.

➤ Such co-operation may include:

✓ Bilateral or multilateral assistance to other countries in the planning, elaboration or implementation of such programmes;

✓ Joint research and peer reviews to improve the quality of the planning and implementation of programmes;

✓ Helping those who work in guidance to acquire knowledge, skill and experience not available in their own countries: for example by giving them access to facilities in other countries or by establishing joint facilities;

✓ The systematic exchange of information, including the results of research and experimental programmes, by means of expert meetings, transnational exchanges and placements, seminars, study groups, thematic networks or exchange of publications; and

✓ The preparation and dissemination of basic guidance material, including curricula and job specifications, to facilitate occupational and geographical mobility.

➤ Member states encourage and support centres that facilitate exchange of experience and promote international co-operation in policy, systems and programme development and methodological research.

OECD PUBLICATIONS, 2, rue André-Pascal, 75775 PARIS CEDEX 16
PRINTED IN FRANCE
(91 2004 02 1 P) ISBN 92-64-01519-1 – No. 53805 2004